A Christmas Carol

Charles Dickens

Notes and activities: Carmel Waldron
Series consultant: Peter Buckroyd

Oxford Literature Companions

OXFORD
UNIVERSITY PRESS

Contents

Introduction

What are Oxford Literature Companions?

Oxford Literature Companions is a series designed to provide you with comprehensive support for popular set texts. You can use the Companion alongside your novella, using relevant sections during your studies or using the book as a whole for revision.

Each Companion includes detailed guidance and practical activities on:

- **Plot and Structure**
- **Context**
- **Characters**
- **Language**
- **Themes**
- **Skills and Practice**

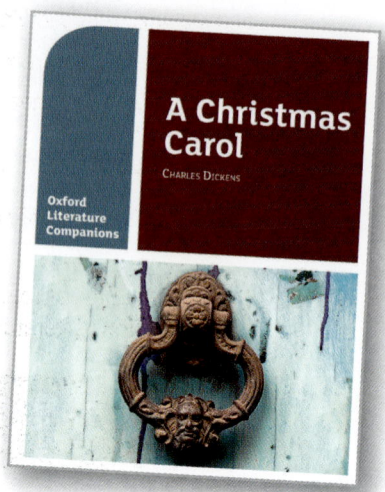

How does this book help with exam preparation?

As well as providing guidance on key areas of the novella, throughout this book you will also find 'Upgrade' features. These are tips to help with your exam preparation and performance.

In addition, in the extensive **Skills and Practice** chapter, the **Exam skills** section provides detailed guidance on areas such as how to prepare for the exam, understanding the question, planning your response and hints for what to do (or not do) in the exam.

In the **Skills and Practice** chapter there is also a bank of **Sample questions** and **Sample answers**. The **Sample answers** are marked and include annotations and a summative comment.

How does this book help with terminology?

Throughout the book, key terms are highlighted in the text and explained on the same page. There is also a detailed **Glossary** at the end of the book that explains, in the context of the novella, all the relevant literary terms highlighted in this book.

How does this book work?

Each book in the Oxford Literature Companions series follows the same approach and includes the following features:

- **Key quotations** from the novella
- **Key terms** explained on the page and linked to a complete glossary at the end of the book
- **Activity boxes** to help improve your understanding of the text
- **Upgrade** tips to help prepare you for your assessment

To help illustrate the features in this book, here are two annotated pages taken from this Oxford Literature Companion:

Key quotations from the novella

Key terms explained on the page and at the end of the book

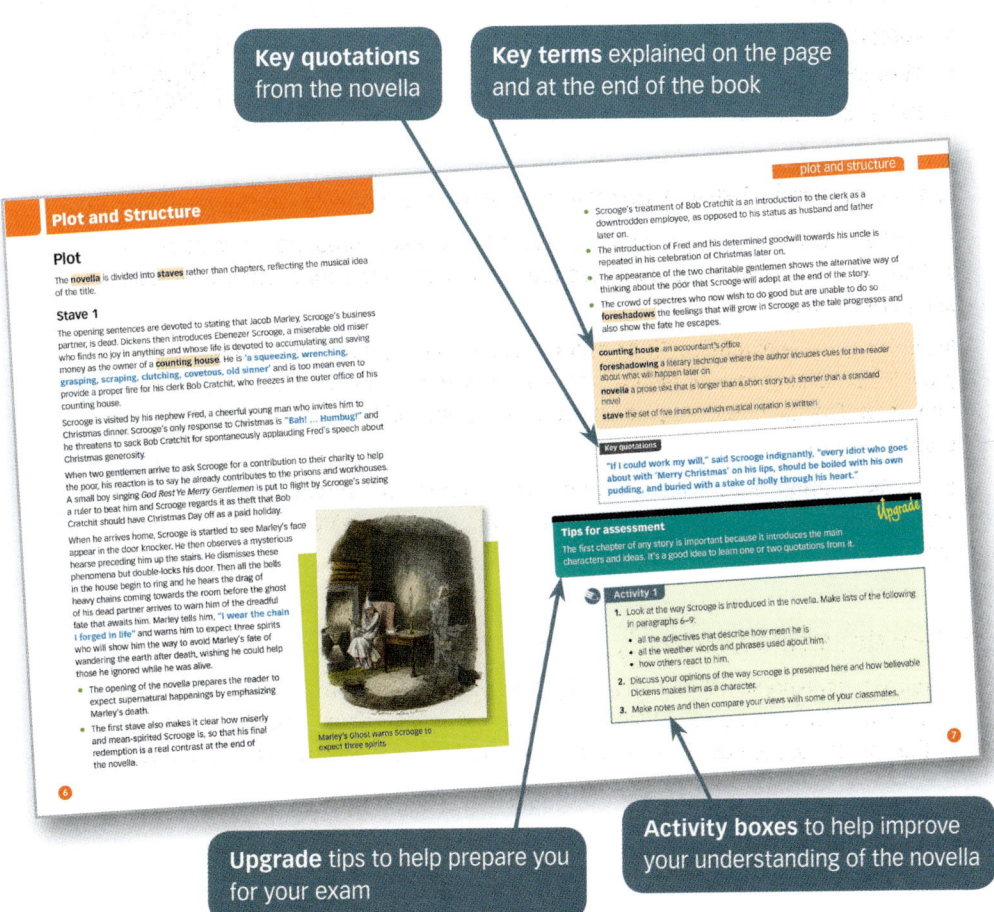

Upgrade tips to help prepare you for your exam

Activity boxes to help improve your understanding of the novella

Plot

The **novella** is divided into **staves** rather than chapters, reflecting the musical idea of the title.

Stave 1

The opening sentences are devoted to stating that Jacob Marley, Scrooge's business partner, is dead. Dickens then introduces Ebenezer Scrooge, a miserable old miser who finds no joy in anything and whose life is devoted to accumulating and saving money as the owner of a **counting house**. He is **'a squeezing, wrenching, grasping, scraping, clutching, covetous, old sinner'** and is too mean even to provide a proper fire for his clerk Bob Cratchit, who freezes in the outer office of his counting house.

Scrooge is visited by his nephew Fred, a cheerful young man who invites him to Christmas dinner. Scrooge's only response to Christmas is **"Bah! ... Humbug!"** and he threatens to sack Bob Cratchit for spontaneously applauding Fred's speech about Christmas generosity.

When two gentlemen arrive to ask Scrooge for a contribution to their charity to help the poor, his reaction is to say he already contributes to the prisons and workhouses. A small boy singing *God Rest Ye Merry Gentlemen* is put to flight by Scrooge's seizing a ruler to beat him and Scrooge regards it as theft that Bob Cratchit should have Christmas Day off as a paid holiday.

When he arrives home, Scrooge is startled to see Marley's face appear in the door knocker. He then observes a mysterious hearse preceding him up the stairs. He dismisses these phenomena but double-locks his door. Then all the bells in the house begin to ring and he hears the drag of heavy chains coming towards the room before the ghost of his dead partner, Jacob Marley, arrives to warn him of the dreadful fate that awaits him. Marley tells him, **"I wear the chain I forged in life"** and warns him to expect three spirits who will show him the way to avoid Marley's fate of wandering the earth after death, wishing he could help those he ignored while he was alive.

Marley's Ghost warns Scrooge to expect three spirits

- The opening of the novella prepares the reader to expect supernatural happenings by emphasizing Marley's death.
- The first stave also makes it clear how miserly and mean-spirited Scrooge is, so that his final redemption is a real contrast at the end of the novella.

- Scrooge's treatment of Bob Cratchit is an introduction to the clerk as a downtrodden employee, as opposed to his status as husband and father later on.
- The introduction of Fred and his determined goodwill towards his uncle is repeated in his celebration of Christmas later on.
- The appearance of the two charitable gentlemen shows the alternative way of thinking about the poor that Scrooge will adopt at the end of the story.
- The crowd of spectres who now wish to do good but are unable to do so **foreshadows** the feelings that will grow in Scrooge as the tale progresses and also show the fate he escapes.

counting house an accountant's office

foreshadowing a literary technique where the author includes clues for the reader about what will happen later on

novella a prose text that is longer than a short story but shorter than a standard novel

stave the set of five lines on which musical notation is written

Key quotations

"If I could work my will," said Scrooge indignantly, "every idiot who goes about with 'Merry Christmas' on his lips, should be boiled with his own pudding, and buried with a stake of holly through his heart."

Tips for assessment

The first chapter of any story is important because it introduces the main characters and ideas. It's a good idea to learn one or two quotations from it.

 Activity 1

1. Look at the way Scrooge is introduced in the novella. Make lists of the following in paragraphs 6–9:
   - all the adjectives that describe how mean he is
   - all the weather words and phrases used about him
   - how others react to him.

2. Discuss your opinions of the way Scrooge is presented here and how believable Dickens makes him as a character. Make notes and then compare your views with some of your classmates.

> ## Activity 2
>
> With a partner, trace the way in which Dickens builds up the mystery and tension towards Marley's eventual appearance. Think about:
>
> - the sequence of events – knocker, hearse, bells, chains, etc.
> - Dickens's use of the senses
> - the language he uses to create a feeling of dread and suspense
> - his use of humour as a disguise for fear
> - the dialogue between Scrooge and Marley when the Ghost does appear.
>
> You could put your findings into a table, if you wish.

Stave 2

Scrooge cannot put Marley's Ghost and its words out of his head, although he tries to dismiss it as a dream. Marley's Ghost bothers him exceedingly: **"Was it a dream or not?"**

The first of the three spirits arrives at one o'clock, as foretold. This is the Ghost of Christmas Past. It is both young and old, summer and winter. It is dressed in white and has a light streaming from its head. It transports Scrooge back to his childhood in the country. He sees boys he remembers playing happily, but is then shown himself as a solitary and neglected child in the schoolroom: **'Scrooge sat down upon a form, and wept to see his poor forgotten self as he used to be'**. Later, he sees his younger sister Fanny, after his father has agreed to let her fetch Scrooge home for good.

The Ghost shows him the office where he was apprenticed as a clerk to Mr Fezziwig, a genial old man, who tells his two apprentices to shut the office early on Christmas Eve and then arranges a dancing party with music and food and drinks for everyone. Scrooge is entranced by this memory and remembers Fezziwig with great fondness.

The scene changes to Scrooge as a more successful man with the beautiful Belle, who is sad that he no longer loves her, because he loves money more. She breaks off their engagement and Scrooge begs the Ghost to spare him any more visions. However, he is forced to watch her happiness with another man and a house full of children.

Scrooge turns on the Ghost, tries to extinguish it with its hat and then falls asleep.

- Dickens shows Scrooge expressing emotion for the first time here, so the reader is now aware that he is capable of feeling.

The Ghost of Christmas Past reminds Scrooge of his lonely childhood

- His neglected and solitary childhood may give the reader a clue as to how he became the man at the start of the story.

- His love of reading and the way the books come alive for him tells us he once had a vivid imagination.

- His fondness for his sister suggests that he may have softer emotions than he has shown so far, while the change in his father foreshadows the change in himself later on.

- His time as an apprentice and his fondness for Fezziwig imply that he once enjoyed Christmas and could have taken a different path. Scrooge's travels with the Ghost are not just through time and space. They are a **metaphor** for his journey through life, showing where he could have made different choices.

> **metaphor** comparison of one thing to another for effect; a metaphor states that one thing is the other, e.g. 'the cold within him froze his old features' *(Stave 1)*

Key quotations

To hear Scrooge expending all the earnestness of his nature on such subjects, in a most extraordinary voice between laughing and crying; and to see his heightened and excited face; would have been a surprise to his business friends in the city, indeed.

Activity 3

1. How does Dickens present the pleasure in Fezziwig's Christmas party?

2. What mood and atmosphere does he create in Belle and her family's celebration of Christmas? How?

3. Why do you think Dickens presents these two Christmas episodes?

4. What effect does each of them have on Scrooge?

Stave 3

Scrooge is rather surprised when no spirit arrives at his bedside on the stroke of one. Instead, he follows a glowing light and finds himself in a transformed version of his own room. He is welcomed by the Ghost of Christmas Present, a jolly giant in a green, furred robe. Scrooge holds the Ghost's robe and finds himself in the streets on Christmas morning. They observe people's good humour as they go about their business, the better off going to church and the poor taking their dinners to be cooked: **'The sight of these poor revellers appeared to interest the Spirit very much, for he stood with Scrooge beside him in a baker's doorway, and taking off the covers as their bearers passed, sprinkled incense on their dinners from his torch'.**

The Ghost then takes Scrooge to Bob Cratchit's home and shows the family preparing for Christmas dinner, with a goose being cooked at the baker's and the pudding at the wash house. Poor people then did not have ovens, so they took roasts to the local baker. They shared a place for washing clothes, where there was a tub to heat the washing. This is where the puddings would have been boiled. There are two daughters, Belinda and Martha; two younger children; the oldest boy, Peter; and the youngest, Tiny Tim, who is lame and sick. Tiny Tim has been to church with Bob while Mrs Cratchit, Belinda and Peter prepared the food. Their Christmas is a merry one, despite their poverty, and Scrooge sees his clerk in a new light. Scrooge finds he is anxious to know if Tiny Tim will live, but the Ghost tells him that if nothing changes he will die, and quotes Scrooge's own words, **"If he be like to die, he had better do it, and decrease the surplus population"**. Scrooge is ashamed and then Bob Cratchit proposes a toast to his employer. The family drink it very reluctantly and with lower spirits than before, although they regain their cheerfulness before Scrooge has to leave.

The Ghost takes Scrooge through streets full of cheerful people hurrying to parties, but then beyond the city to a miner's dwelling, a lighthouse and a boat at sea. In all these places people are celebrating Christmas as best they can.

They then visit the house of Scrooge's nephew, Fred, where there is a big party in progress and everyone is happy and enjoying themselves. Scrooge hears himself being discussed as a miserable miser who gets no satisfaction from his life and benefits neither himself nor anyone else. His nephew says he feels sorry for him as he is the only loser by his attitude. The family and their friends play games, flirt, eat, drink and enjoy themselves very much. Scrooge is so carried away that he tries to join in the games and has time to hear his health being drunk before the Ghost takes him away.

The Ghost tells Scrooge its life ends at the close of the day, since it will no longer be Christmas Present. His final revelation is that he has two children in his robe. They are hideous creatures, shrivelled and ugly. The Ghost tells Scrooge that they are Ignorance and **Want**, and are the children of mankind. He tells Scrooge to beware of them and, when Scrooge asks if they have no refuge, says, **"Are there no prisons?" said the Spirit, turning on him for the last time with his own words. "Are there no workhouses?"**

Scrooge watches the Cratchits at home

- Dickens shows the Ghost of Christmas Present surrounded by plenty and with a torch shaped like a **cornucopia**. This points out the difference between what Scrooge could have and what he does have, shown by the transformed room.

- Dickens shows the Cratchits' house as another contrast between Scrooge and the poor clerk, who has very little but still keeps a merry household and shows generosity by toasting his grudging employer. The softening of Scrooge is revealed in his concern for Tiny Tim.

- The Ghost shows Scrooge that, even in the most miserable and wild places, people still keep the feast in their own way and remember the good will it brings. This is an example to Scrooge, who could afford to live in comfort but chooses not to. Dickens is showing that despite widespread poverty, Christmas goodwill and a generous spirit are universal.

- The cheerful party at Fred's house shows Scrooge what he has rejected. We see his changing attitude as he tries to join in the games.

- Dickens shows the ugly nature of the children who **personify** Ignorance and Want, and uses the now aged Ghost to warn Scrooge what they do to society. The beginnings of change are shown in Scrooge's new desire to know if he can help.

> **Key quotations**
>
> **Scrooge started back, appalled. Having them shown to him in this way, he tried to say they were fine children, but the words choked themselves, rather than be parties to a lie of such enormous magnitude.**

cornucopia the horn of plenty, full of a surplus of good things

personify to give human characteristics to inanimate or abstract ideas or things, e.g. 'Nature lived hard by, and was brewing on a large scale' *(Stave 1)*

want a lack of the most basic essentials of life, such as food, shelter and education

Activity 4

With a partner, examine the section that begins with the description of the second spirit and ends with his sprinkling plenty on the dinners of the poor as they take them to the baker's.

a) Find three examples of each of the following:

- Dickens's use of the sense of sight
- Dickens's use of the sense of hearing
- Dickens's use of the sense of touch
- Dickens's use of the sense of taste.
- Dickens's use of the sense of smell

b) Discuss and make notes on how each example appeals to a particular sense.

c) Write two or three paragraphs on the effect of all this sensual imagery.

Activity 5

1. With a partner, look at the way Dickens shows Scrooge beginning to regret his behaviour and to change his attitude, e.g. in:

    - his reaction to his own words quoted by the Ghost
    - his attitude to the Cratchit family
    - his behaviour at Fred's house
    - his reaction to the two children under the Ghost's cloak.

2. In a small group, take it in turns to take the 'hot seat' as Scrooge. Each of the other group members may ask one question carefully designed to show what Scrooge has learned. The student playing Scrooge must answer in character.

    Questions should be open to allow the character to talk, such as 'How did you feel when...?' or 'What did you think about...?'

Stave 4

The Ghost of Christmas Yet To Come is a figure shrouded in black, with only a hand showing. Scrooge kneels because **'its mysterious presence filled him with a solemn dread'**. It doesn't speak but points the way forward. Scrooge is, by now, very willing to find out what it has to teach him and follows it into the city. He listens to a group of men at the Stock Exchange with whom he is familiar. They are discussing the death of a colleague that nobody cared for and are reluctantly volunteering to arrange a funeral as there is no one else to do it. He then hears two men in the street, who dismiss the death of 'Old Scratch' in between social engagements.

The Ghost then leads Scrooge to the worst area of the city, where poverty and crime are rife. In a low second-hand shop are gathered a **charwoman**, a **laundress** and an undertaker's man. They have goods to sell and they discuss the dead man from whom they have taken them, saying that if he'd had the least humanity he would not have died alone, with no one to care for him and stop his death bed being robbed: **"This is the end of it, you see! He frightened every one away from him when he was alive, to profit us when he was dead! Ha, ha, ha!"** Then the Ghost shows him a corpse on a bed without even curtains round it. It motions him to turn down the sheet, but Scrooge becomes scared and thinks his own life might be going that way. He begs the Ghost to show him someone who shows emotion at the death.

The Ghost shows him a young couple who owed payments on their mortgage to the man, who had refused them even a week's extension on the loan. Their feelings at his death are relief and something like pleasure at the respite it will give them. Scrooge begs the Ghost to show him a death where people feel grief and tenderness, and he is conducted to Bob Cratchit's house, where Bob's wife and daughters are making a shroud for Tiny Tim to be buried in. Bob comes home and tells them he has seen the burial place and has met Scrooge's nephew, who was very kind to him.

Scrooge wants to know where he himself is at this time, but when the Ghost shows him his office it has changed and another person occupies his chair. The Ghost hurries him to the graveyard to show him who the wretch is that was so ill-spoken of and died friendless and alone. On the gravestone, he reads 'Ebenezer Scrooge'.

Scrooge is desperate to know if what he has been shown is inevitable, or only what will happen if he doesn't change: **"Assure me that I yet may change these shadows you have shown me, by an altered life!"** He grabs the Ghost's hand and it dwindles down into a bedpost.

The spirit shows Scrooge his own gravestone

- Dickens uses the Ghost of Christmas Yet To Come to show what will result from Scrooge's present way of life.

- He shows that the only people whose good opinion Scrooge ever wanted – those with money and status in the city – have no sympathy to waste on a mean-hearted skinflint when he dies.

- His lonely death, unloved and unmourned, is a moral message that he can expect nothing, since he gave nothing.

- Dickens gives a clear warning, through the relief of the young family at their creditor's death, that pleasure may be the only emotion felt by others when Scrooge dies.

- Dickens shows that Scrooge's anxiety for Tiny Tim is justified for, without the help that Bob cannot provide, the little boy dies. Unlike Scrooge, however, he is mourned by a family brought closer by his death.

Key quotations

He lay, in the dark empty house, with not a man, a woman, or a child, to say that he was kind to me in this or that, and for the memory of one kind word I will be kind to him. A cat was tearing at the door, and there was a sound of gnawing rats beneath the hearth-stone. What *they* wanted in the room of death, and why they were so restless and disturbed, Scrooge did not dare to think.

charwoman a cleaner
laundress a woman who washes clothes

Activity 6

1. With a partner, reread Stave 4. Without realizing it, Scrooge is hearing what others think about his death. Discuss and make notes on the viewpoints we are shown from:
   - Scrooge's associates in the city
   - Scrooge's debtors, who owe him money
   - the people who are supposed to look after the body.

2. Why do you think Dickens has the Ghost reveal these reactions to Scrooge?

3. What do you consider are Dickens's reasons for showing the death of Tiny Tim as part of the future?

4. Use your notes to write an article for a student magazine about Dickens's presentation of the future in *A Christmas Carol*.

Activity 7

1. Work in a group of three and divide a sheet of paper into three columns with the headings 'Past', 'Present' and 'Future'. Each person in the group should take a column and make a list of the features of that spirit, including short quotations from the story.

2. Once complete, share your lists with your group. Discuss:
   - the similarities you notice between the three spirits
   - the differences between the spirits
   - why you think Dickens chose to present them in this way and what you think each spirit represents. What is their role or function in the novella?

Tips for assessment

You could make some notes on how Dickens uses the setting and characters in this stave to highlight his concerns about poverty and poor living conditions, especially if your exam board assesses context.

Stave 5

Scrooge is overjoyed to find that he is at home in his own bed. He gives thanks to Jacob Marley for his warning and is determined he will be a different person. He hears the church bells and asks a boy outside his window what day it is. When the boy tells him it is Christmas Day, he is delighted he hasn't missed it. He sends the boy to buy a huge turkey he has seen at the butcher's, intending to deliver it anonymously to Bob Cratchit. Then he puts on his best clothes and goes out with a huge smile on his face. He meets one of the men whose request for a donation to the poor he had rejected. He offers him a large donation to make up for all his previous refusals. He then goes to church and afterwards makes his way to his nephew's house, where he is welcomed and thoroughly enjoys himself.

Scrooge is delighted to find out that he hasn't missed Christmas Day

The next morning he decides to play a trick on Bob Cratchit, waiting until he comes in late and then pouncing as if he means to sack him. Instead, he raises Bob's salary and promises to help his family, asking him to buy more coal for the fires and saying, **"we will discuss your affairs this very afternoon, over a Christmas bowl of smoking bishop, Bob"**.

Scrooge is better than his word, **'and to Tiny Tim, who did NOT die, he was a second father'**. He becomes a good man, a good employer and his heart is full of laughter.

Key quotations

He went to church, and walked about the streets, and watched the people hurrying to and fro, and patted children on the head, and questioned beggars, and looked down into the kitchens of houses, and up to the windows, and found that everything could yield him pleasure.

 Activity 8

1. Divide a sheet of paper as below. In the first column find a quotation from early in Stave 1, and in the second find a quotation that shows the difference in Scrooge in Stave 5. The first one has been done for you.

Before	After
"What right have you to be merry? What reason have you to be merry?" (Stave 1)	"I am as light as a feather, I am as happy as an angel" (Stave 5)

2. Discuss and make notes on how Dickens presents Scrooge at the beginning and end of the story. Compare your findings with others in the class.

Tips for assessment

You should be able to show that you understand how the story of *A Christmas Carol* is the story of Scrooge. It tells how the power of compassion and kindness overcomes the evil of selfish materialism.

Activity 9

1. Write five short character profiles of Scrooge. The first profile should describe the presentation of Scrooge in Stave 1, the second should describe his character in Stave 2, and so on. Include some short quotations from the novella in your profiles, such as those below.

    -   "I don't make merry myself at Christmas and I can't afford to make idle people merry." *(Stave 1)*
    -   "There was a boy singing a Christmas Carol at my door last night. I should like to have given him something: that's all." *(Stave 2)*
    -   "Spirit," said Scrooge, with an interest he had never felt before, "tell me if Tiny Tim will live." *(Stave 3)*
    -   "Assure me that I yet may change these shadows you have shown me, by an altered life!" *(Stave 4)*
    -   'His own heart laughed; and that was quite enough for him.' *(Stave 5)*

2. Reread your character profiles. How does Dickens present Scrooge's transformation throughout the novella?

Structure

Dickens's five staves provide the structure of his novella, like five verses of a song (carol) or five stanzas of a poem. Each stave is divided by the ghostly visitation in its title, except for the final one, which is simply called 'The End of It', perhaps referring to the end of the visits, the end of the night, the end of the story or the result of Scrooge's lessons – and probably to all these things.

A Christmas Carol follows a three-act structure, consisting of:

-   the inciting incident (the event that triggers the rest of the plot) – here it is the visit of Marley's Ghost

-   the climax (the event that everything in the novella is building towards) – here it is Scrooge's sight of his grave

-   the resolution (the way everything is tied up at the end) – here it is Scrooge's reformation.

Dickens shapes the novella through the various apparitions that take Scrooge on voyages to the past, present and future:

Stave 1 introduces the reader to Scrooge and shows what he is like. Marley's Ghost provides the inciting incident by warning Scrooge what he can expect if he continues his current behaviour. The Ghost shows Scrooge his heavy chain, forged of the financial instruments he thought so important in his life, and tells Scrooge that his own chain is already much heavier. Scrooge has one last chance to escape the terrible burden. Dickens then uses the fairytale structure of the three Christmas spirits who will help him.

Stave 2 starts to develop the story through the first of the three spirits: the Ghost of Christmas Past. By showing what Scrooge used to be, Dickens uses this Ghost to reveal all the problems and missed opportunities of Scrooge's life so far. This flashback technique gives the reader information about Scrooge's life, while, at the same time, reminding Scrooge that he once had imagination, love and the generosity of an employer. He has abandoned all these in favour of money and the respect of others like himself. Dickens shows the effect of these reminders on Scrooge.

Stave 3 continues the development through the Ghost of Christmas Present, whose voyage stays within the present, but travels widely across land and sea to show the open hearts and generous minds of those who celebrate Christmas, however poor they are and however far away they may be. The Ghost of Christmas Present personifies the goodwill of the season but ends by showing the results of poverty and neglect, and warning that humans ignore them at their peril.

Stave 4 brings the final development through the unspeaking Ghost of Christmas Yet To Come; the future cannot tell us what lies ahead, but death is the inevitable end. Dickens uses a flash-forward as this spirit shows Scrooge what will happen if he continues his current behaviour, leading to the climax when Scrooge sees his name on the neglected gravestone. Whereas Marley's Ghost showed him the torment he could expect after death, this spirit shows how his death would affect the living.

Stave 5 brings the resolution as Dickens shows the result of Scrooge's night travels through time and space, which is also his moral journey from evil skinflint to generous benefactor. Dickens presents a man reborn, one who discovers the joy of giving and the rewards of being pleasant.

Timescale and setting

- There is a dual timescale taking place within the novella: the physical action takes place in a single night, but the metaphorical journey is that of a lifetime.
- Dickens also uses a dual setting technique. The tale is set in London, the city Dickens knew best and where he saw the greatest evils. It is also spread across the country and beyond to show the universal nature of the themes.
- The story is centred around Scrooge's office and his apartment. Scrooge's apartment is the place where his transformation occurs and to where Scrooge returns in between his nocturnal travels.
- The action of the story takes place in one night – Christmas Eve – so that Dickens is able to show Scrooge's change of heart taking place at this season.
- Because the spirits are not bound by time or space, Dickens is able to take Scrooge to many places and have him observe actions over many years. Scrooge himself imagines that days must have passed and is relieved to find that it has all happened in one night.
- The journeys on which Dickens sends Scrooge with the spirits are both physical and mysterious. They appear to take little time, but cover considerable distances.
- These travels are also metaphorical, signifying the emotional and spiritual journey that Scrooge has to undertake in order to become a new person.

Activity 10

1. Work in groups of four.

- Student A should take Staves 1 and 5 and list the settings Dickens uses within them, adding an appropriate quotation for each one.
- Student B should list the different settings of place and time that Dickens uses in Stave 2, with example quotations.
- Student C should list the different settings of place and time that Dickens uses in Stave 3, with example quotations.
- Student D should list the different settings of place and time that Dickens uses in Stave 4, with example quotations.

2. As a group, combine your notes to create a complete list of the different settings and timescales used by Dickens in the novella. Discuss why you think he chose to present his story in this way.

Viewpoint

The story is narrated in the **third person**, although we see mainly Scrooge's point of view. This has the advantage of showing us Scrooge's character from the viewpoint of an **omniscient narrator**, but also shows us how Scrooge feels and thinks. For example, at the start of the story we can see how much the narrator dislikes the **protagonist** by the way he describes him: **'Hard and sharp as flint, from which no steel had ever struck out generous fire; secret, and self-contained, and solitary as an oyster'** *(Stave 1)*. Later we are told, **'The truth is, that he tried to be smart, as a means of distracting his own attention, and keeping down his terror; for the spectre's voice disturbed the very marrow in his bones'** *(Stave 1)*. This implies that the narrator knows what is going on in Scrooge's mind and how he feels about Marley's Ghost.

The narrator also **digresses** to address the reader directly: **'I might have been inclined, myself, to regard a coffin-nail as the deadest piece of ironmongery in the trade'** *(Stave 1)*. This is a device popular with Victorian writers, who often made comments that are similar to an 'aside' in a drama script. Dickens uses it to add ironic comments or moral reflections on his own narration.

The narrator, and thus the reader, follows Scrooge throughout the story. We go where he goes and experience what he experiences. The only exception is in Stave 1 where we are told that **'The office was closed in a twinkling, and the clerk, with the long ends of his white comforter dangling below his waist (for he boasted no great-coat), went down a slide on Cornhill, at the end of a lane of boys, twenty times, in honour of its being Christmas Eve, and then ran home to Camden Town as hard as he could pelt, to play at blindman's-buff'** *(Stave 1)*. Other than this glimpse of Bob Cratchit's exit from the office, we are with Scrooge all the time.

The main benefit of this viewpoint is the reader's ability to see every detail of Scrooge's transformation and to understand how it happens. An apparently instant conversion would be impossible to believe without seeing the progress from joyless miser to generous benefactor as it happens.

> **Key quotations**
>
> **Seeing clearly that it would be useless to pursue their point, the gentlemen withdrew. Scrooge resumed his labours with an improved opinion of himself, and in a more facetious temper than was usual with him.** *(Stave 1)*

Activity 11

Look at the paragraph from Stave 1 that begins 'Scrooge took his melancholy dinner...' down to '... mournful meditation on the threshold'.

a) Rewrite this paragraph in the **first person**, as if you were Scrooge, being careful to use only his point of view.

b) Discuss what changes you needed to make to the original extract in order to do this successfully.

c) Why do you think Dickens chose to write *A Christmas Carol* in the third person rather than from Scrooge's first-person point of view? What effect does this have?

digress to leave the main story in order to make a comment or observation related to something in it, which may be a direct address to the reader

first person from the perspective of the main character in the tale, using the pronoun 'I'

omniscient narrator a storyteller who knows what all the characters are doing, saying and thinking

protagonist the main character in a work of fiction

third person from the perspective of a character or voice outside the story, using the pronouns 'he' or 'she'

Writing about plot and structure

Upgrade

You need to know *A Christmas Carol* very thoroughly. Although you may not be questioned directly on the plot of the novella, you need to show that you understand all the key events and why they happen. This doesn't mean you should tell the story, but that you should be able to select events that are relevant to the question.

Remember to use evidence from the text. Your answer should contain a mixture of references and direct quotations. For example, when writing about the structure of the novella and its timescale, you could include the idea of the spirits as supernatural beings for whom time and space are meaningless, and the metaphorical as well as the physical nature of the journeys.

Biography of Charles Dickens

- Dickens was born in 1812, the second of eight children, to John and Elizabeth Dickens. He was a keen reader from a very young age, which must have influenced his choice of career later on.

- In 1824, his father was imprisoned for debt, together with the family, a condition that Dickens made use of in several of his stories. Charles was sent to work in a factory that made shoe blacking, a terrible time for him. He used his childhood experiences in his writing, and his sympathy for children in poverty and their families runs throughout his work. It can be seen in the Cratchits and in the feral children carried by the Ghost of Christmas Present.

Charles Dickens (1812–1870) was famous in his own lifetime and gave readings of his work to huge, enthusiastic crowds

- Later, his father was released, allowing Charles to attend school again. He worked for a while as a clerk, like Bob Cratchit, while learning shorthand in order to become a journalist.

- At 16, Dickens became a reporter for a parliamentary newspaper, which honed his writing skills and perhaps gave him some idea of the workings of government and the law.

- Dickens published his first novel, *The Pickwick Papers*, in 1837 (the year Queen Victoria came to the throne) and it was well received, encouraging him to write several more. Most of his novels were published originally as serials in magazines, which helped their popularity. He published *A Christmas Carol* at his own expense in 1843. It was an immediate success and has never been out of print since then.

- In 1836, Dickens married Catherine Hogarth, with whom he had ten children before their separation in 1858.

- He also had a love affair with Ellen Ternan, an actor. His sympathy for 'fallen women' may have had something to do with this affair and he established a foundation where single mothers and prostitutes could learn a trade while being cared for. He may be showing this when Scrooge sees the elderly spectre trying to help the poor woman with a baby at the end of Stave 1.

- Dickens travelled extensively in Europe and America, where he spoke against the slave trade. He was a champion of what we would call 'human rights' and his works have a strong moral undertone as well as being entertaining. This is shown very clearly in Scrooge's conversion, when he learns the joy of helping others.

- He became the most successful writer in England, with 15 novels and many shorter pieces to his name. He is second only to Shakespeare in his worldwide fame.

- Dickens is known for his passionate defence of the poor and outcast in English society and for his satirical portrayals of the justice system, the social system and class prejudice. Scrooge represents those rich members of society who refuse to help those in poverty and need.

- Charles Dickens died in 1870 and is buried in Poets' Corner in Westminster Abbey.

Tips for assessment

You should only make reference to the author's life if it is relevant to something in the text or helps to explain his intentions in writing *A Christmas Carol*.

Historical and political context

Throughout most of Dickens's adult life, the reigning monarch was Queen Victoria. Britain was the world superpower, with an empire that covered one fifth of the globe, and whose navy ruled the waves and helped to maintain peace throughout most of her reign. Governments alternated between Tories (Conservatives) and Whigs (Liberals). Most members of both Houses of Parliament were landowners and members of the **aristocracy** and **gentry**. The rise of manufacturers, together with various reform acts, saw a gradual extension of the right to vote, which made the House of Commons more representative, although women would have to wait until 1918.

It was a time of change in many ways, driven by the changing economy, which began to rely less on land and agriculture and more on manufactured goods, thanks to the **Industrial Revolution**. New inventions in machinery made factories more productive, while the use of steam engines enabled goods and people to move further and faster on railways and boats. The use of coal rather than wood as fuel gave greater power and helped the process of making iron for bridges, railways, buildings, machines and even boats. This progress saw the rapid expansion of towns – particularly London – as people moved from the countryside in search of work.

> **aristocracy** those with titles and wealth who owned large estates and stately homes, including members of the royal family
>
> **gentry** the social level just below the aristocracy, whose members owned local manor houses and smaller estates, and sometimes mixed with the aristocracy
>
> **Industrial Revolution** the period from the 18th to the 19th century when goods changed from being made by hand to being made by machines in factories

Social context

Childhood

The result of the expansion of manufacturing processes and the need for coal was a market in child labour and the increase of diseases caused by the materials used in the workplace. Children as young as four or five worked for 12 or 14 hours a day in mines and factories, many of them dying of disease or being killed or maimed in accidents. During Dickens's lifetime, their conditions slowly improved with the passing of the **Factory Acts** and the gradual growth of schools, although education did not become compulsory until 1870, the year of Dickens's death. Dickens's own experience of working in a shoe blacking factory made him very aware of the problems of child labour.

The need for proper education was a priority for Dickens, especially after he visited one of the '**Ragged Schools**' that were set up by well-meaning people for the poor. He wrote about his visit:

> The close, low chamber at the back, in which the boys were crowded, was so foul and stifling as to be, at first, almost insupportable. But its moral aspect was so far worse than its physical, that this was soon forgotten. Huddled together on a bench about the room, and shown out by some flaring candles stuck against the walls, were a crowd of boys, varying from mere infants to young men; sellers of fruit, herbs, lucifer-matches, flints; sleepers under the dry arches of bridges; young thieves and beggars – with nothing natural to youth about them: with nothing frank, ingenuous, or pleasant in their faces; low-browed, vicious, cunning, wicked; abandoned of all help but this; speeding downward to destruction; and UNUTTERABLY IGNORANT.

His description of the children of Want and Ignorance in Stave 3 is very similar.

Key quotations

They were a boy and girl. Yellow, meagre, ragged, scowling, wolfish; but prostrate, too, in their humility. Where graceful youth should have filled their features out, and touched them with its freshest tints, a stale and shrivelled hand, like that of age, had pinched, and twisted them, and pulled them into shreds. Where angels might have sat enthroned, devils lurked, and glared out menacing. No change, no degradation, no perversion of humanity, in any grade, through all the mysteries of wonderful creation, has monsters half so horrible and dread. *(Stave 3)*

Children who were unwanted or orphaned were either sent to the **workhouse**, whose conditions Dickens describes in *Oliver Twist*, or to **baby farms**, where their chances of survival were not good. Those who did survive infancy were sold as free or cheap labour to mines, factories or other industries. There was no idea of state responsibility for children's welfare, but there were some charitable schools and foundling hospitals for those who were lucky. Although the young Cratchits are poor, they have loving parents who live within their small means. *A Christmas Carol* was Dickens's response to the Children's Employment Commission Report on the miseries suffered by many poor children. Dickens exposed selfishness and greed as the dominant features of his England.

A ragged, young watercress seller, c.1880

baby farm infants born to single mothers or those unable to care for them were 'fostered' by people (usually women) for a sum of money. The money was not enough to cover the expenses for long and many infants died from neglect

Factory Acts a series of Acts of Parliament that set out the working conditions of children and adults in factories

Ragged School a school for poor children in cities, offering free education and sometimes clothing and food. This was, for many children, the only education they received. The schools offered reading, writing, arithmetic and Bible studies

workhouse originally set up as a place for the able-bodied unemployed, workhouses provided food and shelter in return for hard labour

Activity 1

1. Dickens writes about childhood in many of his novels. Make notes on how children are presented in the following scenes from *A Christmas Carol*:
   - Stave 1 – the child outside Scrooge's office
   - Stave 2 – Scrooge himself as a child
   - Stave 3 – the Cratchit children
   - Stave 4 – the children of the young couple that owed money to the dying Scrooge
   - Stave 5 – the child Scrooge sends to buy the turkey.

   Include quotations from the novella in your notes.

2. Use the library and the Internet to research the lives of children in Victorian 'Ragged Schools' and workhouses.

3. How did Dickens use his knowledge of the conditions of children in Victorian England, as well as his own experiences, to present childhood in *A Christmas Carol*?

Social inequality

Dickens's novella is also an anti-Malthusian tale. **Malthus** was an early economist whose ideas became popular among businessmen who believed in accumulating material wealth and cared little for the welfare of others. Dickens shows his disgust with the Malthusian principle that population will always grow faster than food supply, and will be controlled through disease and starvation. Scrooge speaks to the charity collector using this principle: **"If they would rather die," said Scrooge, "they had better do it, and decrease the surplus population"** *(Stave 1)*. As a social commentator, Dickens saw the need for the reform of English society; he urged that the wealthy and privileged exhibit greater **humanitarianism** towards the poor and vulnerable.

In a letter to his friend Wilkie Collins dated 6 September 1858, Dickens writes of the importance of social commitment:

> Everything that happens [...] shows beyond mistake that you can't shut out the world; that you are in it, to be of it; that you get yourself into a false position the moment you try to sever yourself from it; that you must mingle with it, and make the best of it, and make the best of yourself into the bargain.

humanitarianism a viewpoint or philosophy that extends compassion and the relief of suffering to all people regardless of nationality, age, gender or religion

Malthus a respected academic and economist who argued that the growth of the world's population would outstrip its ability to provide food for everyone, leading to enforced population control through starvation and disease

Activity 2

You have been asked to write a ten-minute slot for a radio programme about the new wealth and poverty brought by the Industrial Revolution. Your contribution is about how Dickens presented the effects of this in *A Christmas Carol*. You should include points such as:

- how men like Scrooge and Marley became wealthy through financial dealings in stocks and shares, as well as loans
- the lack of protection for workers, especially children, and the long hours and poor pay (think of the Cratchits)
- the fear of being in debt and unable to pay, as this would mean prison (like Caroline and her husband)
- the lack of education and protection for children in poverty (as Ignorance and Want)
- the effects of poverty on families like the Cratchits (Tiny Tim, their clothes, their Christmas dinner, their 'glassware', etc.)
- the effect of poverty on less scrupulous people (like the charwoman and laundress)
- the living conditions of the poor compared with those of the rich.

You could finish on the difference Scrooge was able to make when he cared.

Include brief readings and quotations from the novella.

Poverty and crime

The Victorians were very worried about crime rates, which were extremely high. Penalties included death, transportation and prison, often with hard labour, such as working the treadmill, breaking rocks or picking **oakum**. This is what Scrooge has in mind in Stave 1 when the charity collectors ask him to contribute. Of course, it is hard to separate crime from poverty and while people like Dickens saw that extreme poverty led to crime, others, like Scrooge, merely branded all the poor as criminals and treated them accordingly.

Key quotations

"Are there no prisons?" asked Scrooge.

"Plenty of prisons," said the gentleman, laying down the pen again.

"And the Union workhouses?" demanded Scrooge. "Are they still in operation?"

"They are. Still," returned the gentleman, "I wish I could say they were not."

"The Treadmill and the Poor Law are in full vigour, then?" said Scrooge.

"Both very busy, sir."

"Oh! I was afraid, from what you said at first, that something had occurred to stop them in their useful course," said Scrooge. "I'm very glad to hear it." *(Stave 1)*

Being in debt was a criminal offence that also led to imprisonment, as Dickens knew from his own family. The family seen as **debtors** to the old miser in Stave 4 would no doubt have been sent to prison had he not died first. Poverty itself was seen as a crime, since the only relief offered was the workhouse – a grim institution that split up families and expected hard labour in return for miserable conditions. This was the only option offered by the **Poor Law** and it seems that many people preferred to die than go to a workhouse, which highlights how dreadful they were.

> **debtor** a person who owes money
>
> **oakum** tar-covered rope used in shipping; it was picked apart by hand to create fibres
>
> **Poor Law** a law in England and Wales, amended in 1834, which meant that the rich no longer had to pay taxes in order to help the poor and those affected by poverty had to go into workhouses, which were little better than prisons

Poverty in Victorian England was caused by a rapid increase in the population: an influx of immigrants from Ireland fleeing the Potato Famine, which had left many of them starving; and the flight from the countryside, where there were fewer jobs, to the towns with their factories. The number of people meant that wages were at rock bottom and if the wage earner became unemployed, there were no savings to tide the family over. People were literally starving to death and children were often thrown out of a crowded home to make their own way on the streets. It is against this background that readers have to judge Bob Cratchit's fear of being sacked. In 1848, there were an estimated 30,000 children roaming the London streets. These are the children personified by Dickens as Ignorance and Want at the end of Stave 3.

Poverty and health

One of the worst consequences of the rapid expansion of towns was illness and disease. Without proper planning, houses were jammed in together, with inadequate sanitation and lacking clean water or fresh air. Whole families might live in a single room, which could be damp and unventilated. If they were lucky, they might share a toilet with the rest of the building. In London, especially, there were open sewers and the rubbish was tipped straight into the Thames, while drinking water was drawn from the same stretch of river. It was hardly surprising that tuberculosis was endemic and there were frequent outbreaks of cholera. In the poorer areas of London, one child in five died before their fifth birthday. Such an area is described by Dickens in Stave 4.

The President of the Local Government Board inspects living conditions in London's slums in 1883

> **Key quotations**
>
> **The ways were foul and narrow; the shops and houses wretched; the people half-naked, drunken, slipshod, ugly. Alleys and archways, like so many cesspools, disgorged their offences of smell, and dirt, and life, upon the straggling streets; and the whole quarter reeked with crime, with filth, and misery.** *(Stave 4)*

Even in decent homes there was high child mortality, so for a poor clerk like Bob Cratchit the possibility of buying treatment for Tiny Tim was out of the question. There was no state provision for the sick, and doctors and hospitals charged fees for treatment and medicines. There were charitable foundations that gave help to the poor and sick, like those to whom Scrooge refuses a donation in Stave 1, but they could only provide relief for a few of all those who needed it.

The use of coal as the main fuel added to the health problems of a city where chimneys poured pollution into the sky. The smog described below was common in Victorian London and caused illnesses such as bronchitis and asthma.

> **Key quotations**
>
> **The fog came pouring in at every chink and keyhole, and was so dense without, that although the court was of the narrowest, the houses opposite were mere phantoms. To see the dingy cloud come drooping down, obscuring everything, one might have thought that Nature lived hard by, and was brewing on a large scale.** *(Stave 1)*

Class inequality

In general, Victorian society was divided into classes – upper, middle and lower (or working) class – although there were many changes throughout the 19th century. This class division was partly by wealth, partly by education and partly by occupation. The upper class consisted of landowners who were mainly the aristocracy and gentry, all of whom (the males at least) had attended public schools and then either Oxford or Cambridge University. They were the ruling class who filled seats in Parliament and held the top jobs in the judiciary, the Church and the armed forces. They were often, but not always, the wealthiest members of society.

The middle class was a wide spread, including professionals such as lawyers, doctors, the clergy and army officers, through factory and business owners and engineers, to bank managers, accountants and financiers like Scrooge. Many of the middle class were very wealthy and some attended public schools or sent their sons to them.

The working class included those who worked as teachers, civil servants, shopkeepers, clerks like Bob Cratchit, and skilled and unskilled labourers. They were the largest class and the one with the least economic and political power.

Beneath these was an underclass of criminals, prostitutes and slum dwellers, like that shown by Dickens in Stave 4.

Activity 3

1. Examine the portrait of London that Dickens paints in the novella. Make brief notes on each of the following:

   - the weather
   - street life around Scrooge's office and apartment
   - street life as shown in Stave 3
   - street life in the slums as shown in Stave 4.

2. Prepare a PowerPoint presentation on the London of *A Christmas Carol*, exploring the different facets of society that are portrayed. You should use appropriate quotations from the text and add pictures if you wish. Present it to your class when you have finished or put it on the school intranet.

Victorian Christmas and religious belief

In the early part of the 19th century, Christmas was not celebrated as extensively as it is today and many factories and workplaces were open as usual, which may account for Scrooge's reluctance to give his clerk the whole day off. Queen Victoria and Prince Albert enjoyed celebrating the feast, however, and this meant the custom spread. By the time Dickens wrote his novella, the custom of celebrating Christmas was well established in England.

A middle-class Victorian Christmas

Although the medieval traditions of decorating the house with evergreens and bringing in the Yule log had always been practised, it was the Victorians who put the family at the centre of the Christmas celebration. This was partly because they wanted to be seen as a very moral, church-going society and thought the birth of Jesus should be central to the feast named after him. Scrooge's nephew refers, in Stave 1, to **"the veneration due to its sacred name and origin"** and Tiny Tim, in Stave 3, is hopeful that people will remember the miracles worked by Jesus when they see him in church.

While these two characters are genuinely devout, there are others who are hypocritical or puritan in their outlook, like those mentioned by Scrooge in Stave 3, who want to close everything down on Sundays, but do not consider the hardship this may cause to the poor. There were many others who thought God had given the poor their place in society and they shouldn't complain. These people were also often against educating the poor because they feared that it would make them dissatisfied with their lives.

The custom of coming together as a family for a Christmas feast and a social event was important to the Victorians and this idea is central to *A Christmas Carol*. The practice of attending church on Christmas Day was also seen as essential, and is practised by Bob Cratchit and even Scrooge himself after his conversion. One of Scrooge's few good points is that he is not a hypocrite, unlike those who go to church but do not practise charity in their everyday lives.

Christianity in various forms was practised by Victorian society as a whole. The major religion was Church of England, which was undergoing an **evangelical revival** at the time. These reforms stemmed from the belief that practising good deeds was as important as being devout.

There was also a great interest in **spiritualism** in Dickens's day, which he uses in the episode where Marley's Ghost visits Scrooge. Dickens himself was cynical about it, exposing many mediums as frauds attempting to extract money from a gullible public. He wrote in a letter, 'Although I shall be ready to receive enlightenment from any source, I must say I have very little hope of it from spirits who express themselves through mediums; as I have never yet observed them to talk anything but nonsense'.

> **evangelical revival** the reforming of the Church by people who thought it was important to read the Bible and practise good works
>
> **spiritualism** a belief that the spirits of the dead continue to evolve and that it is possible to communicate with them through gifted 'mediums'

Activity 4

Charles Dickens was a practising Christian and he shows church-going as part of the Christmas celebration. He was also in favour of the virtues of generosity and compassion, along with being able to have a good time. How far are his attitudes seen in the following characters:

- Scrooge's nephew Fred?
- Fezziwig?
- Belle and her family?
- Bob Cratchit?

Write brief notes on how each of these characters can be seen as 'religious' or virtuous in their views and behaviour.

Writing about context

Upgrade

This context section is to help you understand the novella and Dickens's reasons for writing it. You will not be expected to include contextual information in your answer unless it is helpful to the point you are making. It is also important to remember that you should not include much contextual information in your assessment response unless that is one of the assessment objectives for your exam board.

If you need to show that you have understood the author's intentions, then a brief reference only is required. For example, 'Martha Cratchit's need to work as a 'poor apprentice' would have been understood by Dickens, who had a much worse job himself as a child'. However, a whole paragraph about Dickens's boyhood and work would gain no more marks.

Main characters

Ebenezer Scrooge

Dickens introduces Scrooge to the reader as a man whose emotions are frozen and who seems be without humanity: **'The cold within him froze his old features, nipped his pointed nose, shrivelled his cheek, stiffened his gait; made his eyes red, his thin lips blue; and spoke out shrewdly in his grating voice. A frosty <mark>rime</mark> was on his head, and on his eyebrows, and his wiry chin'** *(Stave 1)*.

Scrooge's ruthlessness is demonstrated in his business dealings and he is portrayed as heartless and cruel when, in reply to the charity collectors, he remarks, **"If they [the poor] would rather die," said Scrooge, "they had better do it, and decrease the surplus population"** *(Stave 1)*. He is presented, at the outset, as a man with little or no imagination and therefore no <mark>empathy</mark> for others, since he cannot imagine what it would be like to be them. His refusal to celebrate Christmas is a rejection of what it symbolizes: joy, kindness and generous good fellowship. Scrooge prefers darkness and solitude to light and cheerful company.

The spirits frighten Ebenezer Scrooge

Scrooge also seems to possess a savage sense of humour. His comment about those who enjoy Christmas being boiled with their own pudding and buried with a stake of holly through their hearts has a certain wit about it, even while being curmudgeonly. His reaction to Marley's Ghost is also humorous since, instead of being terrified, he asks if the spectre is able to sit down and then suggests that it may well be the product of **"an undigested bit of beef, a blot of mustard, a crumb of cheese, a fragment of an underdone potato. There's more of gravy than of grave about you, whatever you are!"** *(Stave 1)*.

Dickens uses the character of Scrooge to represent the wealthier members of society who continued to make money at the expense of the poor, without any consideration of their social responsibilities. This lesson is what Scrooge must learn from the spirits when his former partner gives him the opportunity to redeem himself. The first hint that this may be working is when he sees himself as a child. The memory of his lonely and neglected childhood has a powerful effect on Scrooge and also on the reader, who begins to feel some sympathy for him. Dickens shows an imaginative child, too, as the characters in his reading books seem to come alive.

The reminder of his days as an apprentice to Fezziwig have a different effect on Scrooge as he watches the festivities laid on by his former employer. When the Ghost comments that it had cost Fezziwig very little for the entertainment, the reader is surprised to hear Scrooge point out that an employer can make life better or worse for his employees, highlighting the contrast between himself and Fezziwig. This **antithesis** is further explored through Dickens's metaphorical use of darkness. Scrooge, shrouded in physical and moral darkness, watches the **'positive light'** that **'appeared to issue from Fezziwig's calves'** *(Stave 2)*. This is the moment, perhaps, that Scrooge remembers the importance of things other than money, a lesson that is forced home by the Ghost showing him the painful breaking of his engagement and everything he missed as a result. This voyage into his own memory begins the process of reform, as Scrooge realizes the effects of the choices he has made.

The lessons that Scrooge learns from the spirits gradually break down the barriers of greed and selfishness that he has built over the years. The sight of Belle with her daughter reminds him that she could have been his, just as the sight of the Cratchit family shows him that happiness is not dependent on money, but on love. The Ghost of Christmas Present shows Scrooge the universal nature of the celebration. Scrooge even becomes concerned for Tiny Tim: **"Spirit," said Scrooge, with an interest he had never felt before, "tell me if Tiny Tim will live"** *(Stave 3)*. He has the grace to feel ashamed as the Ghost reminds him of his own dreadful words, just as he does when presented with the feral children in the Ghost's robe. The reader is aware of his new interest in their fate: he has clearly never considered, or cared, what his unpleasant comments might mean in reality.

When the Ghost whisks him into his nephew's family Christmas party, Dickens shows Scrooge starting to understand what it means to be happy in the company of others and trying to join in the games. This is the opposite of the man who was so rude to his nephew and refused to join him for Christmas dinner, and shows the Christmas spirit beginning to change Scrooge as he comes into the light.

antithesis contrast or opposite
empathy the ability to understand someone else's feelings
rime deposit of frost

In contrast to the other spirits, the Ghost of Christmas Yet To Come works through fear. The Ghost fills Scrooge with dread and shows the inevitable end of all human life. For Scrooge, the ending seems grim indeed as he is shown a corpse without a single mourner, left to the rats and the human vultures that strip it of everything but a single sheet. He is shown reactions to the death that range from indifference to relief, which is contrasted with the passing of Tiny Tim. Finally, Scrooge is terrified that he will die before he has the chance to redeem himself. Most of this stave takes place in darkness, a state that Scrooge no longer wants to live in.

His relief at finding it is still Christmas morning is presented along with his newfound desire to celebrate Christmas in the right spirit. Dickens portrays Scrooge behaving like a child: **"I don't know what day of the month it is!" said Scrooge. "I don't know how long I've been among the Spirits. I don't know anything. I'm quite a baby. Never mind. I don't care. I'd rather be a baby. Hallo! Whoop! Hallo here!"** *(Stave 5)*. This suggests he has been reborn as a new man. It provides a stark contrast with his depiction as aged and shrivelled in Stave 1, and shows that the inner child who imagined characters from books as alive and the young apprentice who revelled in Fezziwig's party are still there, buried deep inside. Scrooge has a new interest in those around him and begins to discover the joy of helping others.

The miserable old skinflint of Stave 1 has undergone a ==metamorphosis== and, through a process of remembering and seeing the lives of others in detail, as well as fearing what might become of himself, he has started to behave in a more compassionate manner. He has learned to enjoy himself and to empathize with others, and become a benefactor. He can hardly wait to see Bob Cratchit and give him a rise in salary and we are told that he helps the family, especially Tiny Tim. By the end of the novella, he has become a model of a good person: **'... it was always said of him, that he knew how to keep Christmas well, if any man alive possessed the knowledge. May that be truly said of us, and all of us! And so, as Tiny Tim observed, God bless Us, Every One!'** *(Stave 5)*.

Dickens often uses metaphors to present Scrooge's character. At the beginning of the story, he is shown in terms of bad weather – frost, rain, wind and hail: **'Foul weather didn't know where to have him'** *(Stave 1)*. His moral state is shown through the metaphor of fog, which obscures his vision, creating a spiritual darkness. Unlike the people who gather round braziers, or the lighted shops, Scrooge deprives his clerk, and himself, of light and warmth, the ==symbols== of clear vision and compassion.

The language used to describe Scrooge changes after his redemption, when the weather becomes sunny and clear and he is seen in terms of laughter: Scrooge manages a **'splendid laugh'** *(Stave 5)*, although out of practice. Dickens then describes him sending the Cratchits a turkey in a sentence that contains the word 'chuckle' six times to emphasize Scrooge's newfound delight in giving. Dickens also uses an ==accumulation of clauses== within a fast-moving sentence to show Scrooge's zest for life: **'He went to church, and walked about the streets, and watched** the people hurrying to and fro, and patted children on the head, and questioned beggars, and looked down into the kitchens of houses, and up to the windows, and found that everything could yield him pleasure' *(Stave 5).*

Key quotations

But what did Scrooge care! It was the very thing he liked. To edge his way along the crowded paths of life, warning all human sympathy to keep its distance, was what the knowing ones call 'nuts' to Scrooge. *(Stave 1)*

He became as good a friend, as good a master, and as good a man, as the good old city knew, or any other good old city, town, or borough, in the good old world. *(Stave 5)*

---

accumulation of clauses a building up of clauses, one after another; a clause is a part of a sentence that includes a subject and verb and could stand on its own

metamorphosis one thing changing into another; a transformation

symbol an object used to represent an idea, e.g. a flag has a symbolic meaning as the representation of a country

---

Activity 1

Look at the two key quotations about Scrooge above. One is taken from the beginning of the novella and the other from the end.

How is he presented differently at the beginning and end of the novella? Consider:

- the language Dickens uses to describe Scrooge in Stave 1 and Stave 5
- the way he is shown behaving in Stave 1 and Stave 5
- the things he says and the way he says them in Stave 1 and Stave 5
- how other people react to him in Stave 1 and Stave 5.

Write four paragraphs outlining how Dickens presents Scrooge's transformation, including quotations from the novella and using the points above to help you.

Tips for assessment

You need to be able to write about the character as presented by the author. This means you should show understanding of the way Dickens uses language to show speech and behaviour, and also how he uses metaphor to suggest the moral side of a person.

Bob Cratchit

On our first introduction to Bob Cratchit we are immediately aware that he is very put upon. Scrooge has little concern for his comfort. Dickens's metaphorical description of the room as **'a sort of tank'** suggests Bob is in full view, while the word **'cell'** implies he is a prisoner *(Stave 1)*. He is freezing because he is not allowed a proper fire and threatened with the sack for agreeing with Fred about Christmas. Despite his hardships and low wages, he makes the best of things and greets Fred cheerfully. His exuberant behaviour as he **'went down a slide on Cornhill, at the end of a lane of boys'** *(Stave 1)* shows that, unlike his employer, Bob Cratchit has not lost touch with his inner child.

Bob Cratchit with his son Tiny Tim

Bob is not only a clerk; he is a husband and the father of six children. Like Bob, the family are caring and generous, and make the best of what little they have. Dickens shows a family where love and kindness matter far more than material goods. Bob's open nature is shown in the way he toasts Scrooge as **"the Founder of the Feast"** *(Stave 3)*, despite being treated so badly by his employer. When Dickens shows a future where Tiny Tim has died, Bob's grief is shown alongside his love for his wife and his care for the family, as well as his gratitude to Fred for being kind to him. At Scrooge's office, Bob is shown in cold and darkness, while at home he is shown in light and warmth: **'Bob served it out with beaming looks, while the chestnuts on the fire sputtered and cracked noisily'** *(Stave 3)*.

Dickens uses Bob Cratchit and his family as an example of people living in poverty, who nevertheless create a loving home and behave with honest dignity. They enjoy their Christmas in spite of the sadly inadequate 'feast' because they are together. They form a contrast to Scrooge, who prefers to be alone and has no room in his life for others. By the end of the story, however, Scrooge has almost adopted them, having realized his clerk's true worth. Bob Cratchit gets his just reward in an increased salary and the promise that Scrooge would be a **'second father'** to Tiny Tim *(Stave 5)*.

Key quotations

... in came little Bob, the father, with at least three feet of comforter exclusive of the fringe, hanging down before him; and his threadbare clothe darned up and brushed, to look seasonable; and Tiny Tim upon his shoulder. *(Stave 3)*

Activity 2

1. Dickens shows two different sides to Bob Cratchit: as Scrooge's clerk and as a husband and father. How is he presented in each role?

2. What differences do you notice between Dickens's presentation of Bob Cratchit and his presentation of Scrooge? You should think about:

   - the language he uses to describe each of them
   - the metaphors he uses to reveal their characters
   - their relationships with other characters in the narrative.

Tiny Tim

Dickens introduces Tiny Tim in Stave 3 as he returns from church with his father, who has **'Tiny Tim upon his shoulder. Alas for Tiny Tim, he bore a little crutch, and had his limbs supported by an iron frame!'** *(Stave 3)*. Tiny Tim is presented sympathetically as a young boy with disabilities. He is certainly looked after, for Dickens tells us **'the two young Cratchits hustled Tiny Tim, and bore him off into the wash-house, that he might hear the pudding singing in the copper'** *(Stave 3)*. Although he is not able to be very active, he is seen as a precious member of the family, joining in whenever he can. He contributes to the entertainment as well, singing a song. He is important in Scrooge's reform, as the old miser seems to take an interest in him and his welfare: **'Scrooge had his eye upon them, and especially on Tiny Tim, until the last'** *(Stave 3)*.

His role in the story is to show how poverty can affect those who are ill and unable to pay for treatment. Dickens has chosen to present a child as this makes it easier to gain the reader's sympathy. Victorian readers would have been familiar with childhood illness and death, but Dickens tends to show such children, like Tiny Tim, in an overly sentimental way by making them excessively virtuous, such as when Tim hopes the churchgoers would see him and **"remember upon Christmas Day, who made lame beggars walk, and blind men see"** *(Stave 3)*.

Tiny Tim is a significant character in the story more for the effect he has on others than for his personal qualities. He is close to his family and especially to his father, who **'dreaded that he might be taken from him'** *(Stave 3)*. He causes Scrooge for the first time in his life to consider the effects of poverty on real people who are bound by their own circumstances, and this lesson is remembered when he sees the figures of Ignorance and Want later on.

Tiny Tim's death in Stave 4 has a **salutary** effect on Scrooge, while it brings grief and loss to his family. The knowledge that this death was caused by the lack of money to pay for the necessary treatment contributes to Scrooge's change of heart.

salutary beneficial

Activity 3

Readers tend to have strong reactions to Tim Cratchit, either feeling sympathy for his plight or finding him a bit too good. In a small group, discuss:

- how you feel towards Tiny Tim
- how you think Victorian readers might have felt
- how you think Dickens wanted his readers to feel.

Fred

The reader's first impression of Scrooge's nephew Fred is of someone healthy, happy and alive and a complete contrast to his uncle, particularly in his good will: **'He had so heated himself with rapid walking in the fog and frost, this nephew of Scrooge's, that he was all in a glow; his face was ruddy and handsome; his eyes sparkled, and his breath smoked again'** *(Stave 1)*. He is described as having **'a cheerful voice'** and replies to his uncle's rude remarks **'gaily'** *(Stave 1)*. His speech in defence of Christmas prompts applause from Bob Cratchit, although it makes little impression on Scrooge. Fred is thoughtful enough to stop and speak in a friendly way to the clerk. This ability to empathize with people is typical of Fred, as well as being another point of contrast with Scrooge.

His good nature and benevolence in providing plenty for his guests to eat and drink, amusing stories and party games provides an alternative to Scrooge's isolation. When taken there by the Ghost of Christmas Present, Scrooge loses himself in the party atmosphere and is very sorry to be dragged away. The result, in Stave 5, is that he finally plucks up the courage to join his nephew on Christmas Day and, far from reproaching him for his previous lapses, Fred greets him warmly as do his other guests: **'It is a mercy he didn't shake his arm off. He was at home in five minutes'** *(Stave 5)*.

Fred represents the real spirit of Christmas in a human, rather than spirit, form. He is a vital, warm and glowing person who provides an antithesis to his dark and frozen uncle. In contrast to Scrooge's refusal to help the poor, he enquires after Bob Cratchit's family and offers to help them in any way he can. He is a link to Scrooge's past because he is the son of his sister, the **'little Fan'** we see in Stave 2. Additionally, the song Scrooge hears in Fred's house reminds him of the girl who loved him and helps to restore his shrivelled emotions.

> **Key quotations**
>
> "I am sure I have always thought of Christmas time, when it has come round – apart from the veneration due to its sacred name and origin, if anything belonging to it can be apart from that – as a good time; a kind, forgiving, charitable, pleasant time; the only time I know of, in the long calendar of the year, when men and women seem by one consent to open their shut-up hearts freely, and to think of people below them as if they really were fellow-passengers to the grave, and not another race of creatures bound on other journeys. And therefore, uncle, though it has never put a scrap of gold or silver in my pocket, I believe that it *has* done me good, and *will* do me good; and I say, God bless it!" *(Stave 1)*

Activity 4

1. Look at the quotations below. Discuss what each one suggests about Fred's character.

   - "I want nothing from you; I ask nothing of you; why cannot we be friends?" *(Stave 1, to Scrooge)*
   - "If it only puts him in the vein to leave his poor clerk fifty pounds, that's something..." *(Stave 3)*
   - "A Merry Christmas and a Happy New Year to the old man, whatever he is!" *(Stave 3)*
   - "I am heartily sorry for it, Mr. Cratchit," he said, "and heartily sorry for your good wife." *(Stave 4)*
   - "If I can be of service to you in any way, … that's where I live. Pray come to me." *(Stave 4, to Bob)*
   - "Let him in! It is a mercy he didn't shake his arm off." *(Stave 5, Scrooge at Fred's)*

2. Use your notes to write a short essay about how Dickens presents Fred.

Jacob Marley

Dickens begins his novella with the fact that **'Marley was dead, to begin with'**, since his story is more concerned with Marley's Ghost and the transformation it sparks in Scrooge, than in the living person who had been Scrooge's partner in business. Marley appears to have had nobody else in his life either: **'Scrooge was his sole executor, his sole administrator, his sole assign, his sole residuary legatee, his sole friend, and sole mourner'** *(Stave 1)*. The repetition of 'sole' here makes it clear that Marley was an isolated figure and there was no one else in his life. Scrooge, however, does have family but chooses to behave as if he were alone. Dickens makes Marley and Scrooge very similar characters, which is necessary for Marley's Ghost to offer authentic-sounding advice to Scrooge and for Scrooge to take it.

Marley's main purpose in the story is to warn Scrooge to change his way of life while he can. The spectre tells him of his dreadful fate in the afterlife, wandering the Earth wishing, but unable, to do the good he neglected in life. Dickens shows him hampered by a long chain **'of cash-boxes, keys, padlocks, ledgers, deeds, and heavy purses wrought in steel'** *(Stave 1)*. He tells Scrooge, **"I wear the chain I forged in life... I made it link by link, and yard by yard; I girded it on of my own free will, and of my own free will I wore it. Is its pattern strange to *you*?"** *(Stave 1)*. Marley's punishment is fitting and his state in the afterlife reflects the misdeeds he committed during his time on Earth.

Jacob Marley's Ghost

The long listing of objects associated with his business indicates the severity of his earthly errors. The repetition of 'free will' shows that it was Marley's own doing. This makes it clear that Scrooge will inevitably follow Marley's fate, unless he can find some way of changing it.

The only good the Ghost has managed to do is to procure a chance for Scrooge, his former partner, to avoid the same fate as himself by being visited by three spirits. Thus Dickens sets up the premise of the haunting through another spirit (Marley), albeit a familiar one that Scrooge will trust.

Key quotations

"Mankind was my business. The common welfare was my business; charity, mercy, forbearance, and benevolence, were, all, my business. The dealings of my trade were but a drop of water in the comprehensive ocean of my business!" *(Stave 1)*

Activity 5

Work with a partner.

1. Divide a page into two columns. Head one column 'Marley's Ghost' and the other 'Scrooge'. Reread the episode where Marley's Ghost visits Scrooge. Put each speech or action of the Ghost in the first column; in the second column put the corresponding reaction in words and actions from Scrooge. (You could use an online version of the novella to copy and paste.)

2. Discuss how Dickens presents Marley's spirit and Scrooge's reactions to it. You should consider:

   - the language the Ghost uses
   - its actions
   - how Dickens describes it
   - how Scrooge reacts to it.

3. Prepare a two-minute speech for the class, or a group, giving your opinion on the importance of this episode to the story. Remember to support your points with references and quotations.

Tips for assessment

You need to show that you understand not only the characters themselves, but also their function in the story – the reason they are there.

The Ghost of Christmas Past

The first of the spirits to visit Scrooge is described as **'like a child: yet not so like a child as like an old man, viewed through some supernatural medium, which gave him the appearance of having receded from the view, and being diminished to a child's proportions. Its hair, which hung about its neck and down its back, was white as if with age; and yet the face had not a wrinkle in it, and the tenderest bloom was on the skin'** (Stave 2). This ancient child is a thing of contradictions, being young and old, winter and summer, white-haired and unwrinkled. The light that shines from its head can be extinguished by its cap and its whole being fluctuates between light and dark. The Ghost of Christmas Past, and its light, represents Memory.

Scrooge's first reaction is to beg the Ghost to wear his cap, indicating that he cannot bear to face the past. The suggestion is that Scrooge has forced the past to remain forgotten, but now the Ghost is about to shed its light upon Scrooge's earlier years. It is Memory that brings back feelings to Scrooge and he sobs as he recalls the neglected boy left alone in school at Christmas time, while the others are out playing together. This Ghost shows the reader the possible reason for Scrooge's dislike of the season, although it is also at this time of year that his little sister comes to take him home. The Ghost seems aware of its effect on him as it **'smiled thoughtfully'** *(Stave 2)* when Scrooge wishes he hadn't chased away the carol singer in Stave 1. The Ghost chooses its memories carefully, selecting those that are most likely to affect Scrooge and his future behaviour. It reminds him, for example, that his nephew is the child of that little sister.

The Ghost's light seems to reflect the clarity of Scrooge's memories, for after the Christmas party at Fezziwig's **'the light upon its head burnt very clear'** *(Stave 2)*. It also provokes Scrooge into thinking in a different way from usual, for when it points out **"He has spent but a few pounds of your mortal money: three or four perhaps. Is that so much that he deserves this praise?"** *(Stave 2)*. Scrooge is quick to reply that it isn't the money that matters, but the fact that Fezziwig chose to make his clerks happy rather than miserable, when he had the power to do either. The Ghost then shows him the memory of his broken engagement and the reason for it, but refuses to stop at this: **'But the relentless Ghost pinioned him in both his arms, and forced him to observe what happened next'** *(Stave 2)*. Scrooge seems distressed by the memory of what could have been and tries to extinguish the Ghost. This indicates to the reader that his long buried feelings are coming to the surface again.

Scrooge with the Ghost of Christmas Past

Key quotations

The Spirit dropped beneath it, so that the extinguisher covered its whole form; but though Scrooge pressed it down with all his force, he could not hide the light, which streamed from under it, in an unbroken flood upon the ground. *(Stave 2)*

Work with a partner and choose one of the following:

1. Find two or three different film versions of *A Christmas Carol* online. Find the scene with the Ghost of Christmas Past in each one.

   For each version, compare it with the description in the novella. Use the prompts below to guide you.

   - Discuss how far it is similar or different from Dickens's presentation?
   - Can you see why the film director has chosen to present the Ghost as it is on screen?
   - Which version do you prefer and why?

   Finally, describe how you would present the Ghost of Christmas Past if you were directing a new version of the story.

2. Look carefully at Dickens's description of the Ghost of Christmas Past. List the characteristics that Dickens mentions and, alongside each feature, write down how you think it relates to the idea of memory.

The Ghost of Christmas Present

The Ghost of Christmas Present

Unlike the previous spirit, which came to his bedside, the Ghost of Christmas Present, the second of the three spirits foretold to Scrooge, summons him through a blaze of light. The light here is not that of memory but of knowledge. The transformation of Scrooge's room into a Christmas grotto, overflowing with food, drink and warmth is matched by the Ghost who is 'a jolly Giant, glorious to see; who bore a glowing torch, in shape not unlike **Plenty's horn**, and held it up, high up, to shed its light on Scrooge, as he came peeping round the door' *(Stave 3)*. This apparition invites Scrooge to know him better, as he personifies everything that is generous and giving about Christmas. The Ghost wears a loose green robe and a holly wreath and a disused rusty scabbard from which the sword, a symbol of battle, is missing, implying that it has known peace for

Plenty's horn also known as 'Cornucopia', this is a mythical horn filled with everlasting produce

a very long time. The **"More than eighteen hundred"** brothers of which it speaks *(Stave 3)* are the number of years since Christ's birth – the original Christmas. True to its first appearance, the Ghost takes Scrooge into the streets, where the shops are full of Christmas goods. The people in whom the Ghost takes the most interest, however, are the poorest: those like the Cratchits who have no oven and have to take their dinners to the baker to be cooked: **'The sight of these poor revellers appeared to interest the Spirit very much, for he stood with Scrooge beside him in a baker's doorway, and taking off the covers as their bearers passed, sprinkled incense on their dinners from his torch'** *(Stave 3)*. The torch represents the light of goodwill, for it makes those sprinkled with its contents feel happier and at peace with each other.

Dickens uses the Ghost to criticize those narrow-minded religious people who would like to shut all the bakers and other shops on Sundays, for when Scrooge chides the Ghost for wanting to deprive the poor of their Sunday dinner, he tells Scrooge this is untrue. The Ghost claims that there are some **'who do their deeds of passion, pride, ill-will, hatred, envy, bigotry, and selfishness in our name, who are as strange to us and all our kith and kin, as if they had never lived'** *(Stave 3)*. This spirit seems to speak for the author himself, and against the businessmen and financiers who make money at the expense of the poor. He is like a mentor, sent to teach Scrooge by example and by wise words. This seems even truer when he reveals the children in his robe, the results of poverty and ignorance created by a society that does not care.

Activity 7

1. With a partner, read through Stave 3, finding quotations that support the following character traits of the Ghost of Christmas Present.

   - The Ghost is open and overflowing with generosity.
   - The Ghost is keen to help the poor most of all.
   - The Ghost is against narrow religious views of Sundays that would close bakeries.
   - The Ghost is angry at those who would decree who has a right to live or die.
   - The Ghost is pleased that Scrooge is learning to enjoy himself.
   - The Ghost ages through the course of the night.
   - The Ghost warns Scrooge that poverty and lack of education will be dangerous to society.

   What do your selected quotations reveal about Dickens's presentation of the Ghost of Christmas Present?

2. 'The Ghost of Christmas Present is just a jolly giant, and nothing more.' Discuss this statement with a partner or in small groups. Do you agree or disagree? Give reasons for your answer.

   What do you think this spirit represents in Dickens's time and in modern times?

The Ghost of Christmas Yet To Come

Of the three spirits, the Ghost of Christmas Yet To Come is the one most like a 'traditional' spook: **'The Phantom slowly, gravely, silently, approached. When it came near him, Scrooge bent down upon his knee; for in the very air through which this Spirit moved it seemed to scatter gloom and mystery'** *(Stave 4).* It has a predictable effect on Scrooge; we are told he **'feared the silent shape so much that his legs trembled beneath him, and he found that he could hardly stand when he prepared to follow it'** *(Stave 4).* All this prepares the reader for what will be the darkest part of the story, in the company of a spirit that resembles the figure of the Grim Reaper. Where the first Ghost offered memories, both good and bad, and the second Ghost showed the happiness and goodwill of Christmas, as well as the evils of poverty, this Ghost shows only misery and death. He seems to represent the fear that humans have of death, as well as Scrooge's personal fear of what the afterlife will mean for him, following the appearance of Marley's Ghost.

The Ghost takes him to places and indicates people he should listen to, although Scrooge is puzzled by its motives, **'surprised that the Spirit should attach importance to conversations apparently so trivial'** *(Stave 4).* However, there is an ultimate purpose to the Ghost's behaviour. Its actions in showing first the reactions to Scrooge's death, then the way in which his body is treated and finally the way in which the news is received by his debtors all lead to the final revelation of his own grave and the awful realization of what he might expect in the future.

The Ghost of Christmas Yet To Come looks like the Grim Reaper

The spectre seems relentless and immoveable, yet when Scrooge begs it to say whether he can change the future he has seen, **'For the first time the hand appeared to shake'** *(Stave 4).* This implies that the Ghost is not as implacable as it appears, especially as we read that its hand trembled at Scrooge's pleading for another chance. It leaves Scrooge sobbing violently, testifying to the desperation he feels to have an opportunity to mend his ways. He now realizes the urgency of leaving the cold darkness and coming into the warm light.

Key quotations

It was shrouded in a deep black garment, which concealed its head, its face, its form, and left nothing of it visible save one outstretched hand. But for this it would have been difficult to detach its figure from the night, and separate it from the darkness by which it was surrounded. *(Stave 4)*

Activity 8

How does Dickens present the Ghost of Christmas Yet To Come? You should think about:

- the Ghost's silence and its effect on the reader
- the Ghost's actions
- Scrooge's reactions to the Ghost itself
- **Scrooge's reactions to** what the Ghost shows him.

Fezziwig

Fezziwig, Scrooge's former boss, is a role model for how an employer should behave. He reminds Scrooge of his kindness as an employer and helps him to appreciate that what mattered to him in the past was not how much money was spent, but the spirit in which things were given. The first thing we know about him is his laugh: **'He … laughed all over himself, from his shoes to his organ of benevolence'** *(Stave 2)*. This tells us that he is someone who can enjoy life. This point is then expanded as he jollies his apprentices along to shut the office and make everything ready for his Christmas Eve party. He is the opposite of Marley and of Scrooge himself in his open-handed love of enjoyment. Whereas for Scrooge, **'Darkness is cheap, and Scrooge liked it'** *(Stave 1)*, the reader learns that **'A positive light appeared to issue from Fezziwig's calves'** *(Stave 2).* Fezziwig shows that making money and running a business can be done while remaining an open and generous person who cares about their family and employees. Although Fezziwig only appears in one scene, he is a memorable character.

Key quotations

"He has the power to render us happy or unhappy; to make our service light or burdensome; a pleasure or a toil. Say that his power lies in words and looks; in things so slight and insignificant that it is impossible to add and count 'em up: what then? The happiness he gives, is quite as great as if it cost a fortune." *(Stave 2)*

1. With a partner, look at the way in which Dickens builds up a picture of Fezziwig through his behaviour on a single evening.

   - Start by looking at how Dickens introduces him. What are we told about him first? How does this affect the reader's view of him?
   - Then look at how Dickens shows the relationship between Fezziwig and his apprentices. How does he treat them? How do they respond to him?
   - Look at how Dickens's description of the dancing tells the reader more about Fezziwig. What do we learn about him from his conduct on the dance floor?
   - How does Dickens's presentation of the guests suggest that Fezziwig is open-handed and generous? (You may need to do some close reading here.)
   - What does Fezziwig's manner of saying goodbye to his guests tell us about his character?
   - What do Scrooge's reactions, as he watches, imply about his opinion of his old employer?

2. Write a character profile of Fezziwig, using your findings and including any useful quotations.

The Cratchit family

Bob Cratchit's family provides some of the most attractive characters. Mrs Cratchit, who makes no complaints at wearing her old dress trimmed up with ribbons, is the ideal wife and mother, and is appreciated as such by her husband. She is shown as the proud housekeeper in Stave 3, although her opinions of Scrooge are voiced clearly. She is indignant for her husband, showing her affection and loyalty to him. The Cratchits have fun together at Christmas in spite of having so little. In the later scene, in Stave 4, where Mrs Cratchit is shown sewing a shroud for Tiny Tim, she still thinks of Bob. She tries to comfort her husband although she is grieving herself. After Tiny Tim's death, the family is unusually quiet and the children particularly caring of their father. The Cratchits are shown as a very close and loving family for whom poverty is always present, but who never allow it to divide them or make them bitter. They show that, contrary to what Scrooge believes at the outset of the story, there are loving, hard-working families who are trapped in poverty through no fault of their own. The Cratchit family demonstrates that the poor are not all idle and undeserving, as some sections of Victorian society believed.

> **Key quotations**
>
> **The compound in the jug being tasted, and considered perfect, apples and oranges were put upon the table, and a shovel-full of chestnuts on the fire. Then all the Cratchit family drew round the hearth, in what Bob Cratchit called a circle, meaning half a one; and at Bob Cratchit's elbow stood the family display of glass. Two tumblers, and a custard-cup without a handle.** *(Stave 3)*

Activity 10

In a group of four, reread the scenes in the Cratchit home in Stave 3 and Stave 4.

a) Discuss how Dickens uses language to convey the difference in atmosphere between the two scenes. You should consider the following and select short quotations to illustrate each bullet point.

- Both scenes open with Mrs Cratchit. How does her presentation differ in each case?
- In both scenes the family is waiting for Bob's arrival. What differences are there in attitude and conversation?
- How does the behaviour of the younger Cratchits differ in each scene?
- What differences do you notice in Peter Cratchit each time?
- How is the manner of Bob's arrival different in each scene?
- Are there any similarities between the scenes?

Think about:

- what the characters say
- what the characters do
- how the characters react to each other
- what the narrator says about them.

b) Join with another group and compare your findings. Stage a tableau of each scene in such a way as to show the atmosphere in each case.

Minor characters

Dickens's novella is full of characters, some of which appear very briefly, and others that play a small but significant role in the story. Most of these characters have a symbolic function and reveal more about Scrooge's character and his transformation.

Two of these characters are Scrooge's sister, Fanny, and his ex-fiancée, Belle. These two both try to help Scrooge in his youth.

'Little Fan', as Scrooge calls her, intercedes with her father to allow Ebenezer home, not just for Christmas, but permanently. She is described as **"Always a delicate creature, whom a breath might have withered," said the Ghost. "But she had a large heart!"** (Stave 2). She died young, leaving a boy – Scrooge's nephew, Fred. He feels great affection for her when revisiting his past, but has not extended this love to Fred or his family. Her appearance in the vision reminds him of this.

Along with Scrooge, we see Belle reluctantly breaking their engagement because she says, **"Another idol has displaced me; and if it can cheer and comfort you in time to come, as I would have tried to do, I have no just cause to grieve"** (Stave 2). This idol is money and the reader is made aware that, even when young, Scrooge put the acquisition of wealth before everything, including love. Belle tells him, **"That which promised happiness when we were one in heart, is fraught**

Belle and her family represent a happy life that Scrooge once cast aside for the love of money

with misery now that we are two" *(Stave 2).* She has not changed, but Scrooge has. Belle's role in the story is to remind Scrooge of how he once put love before money and did not care that Belle was poor. This painful reminder is emphasized by the happiness she enjoys with a husband and children who value her properly.

The brief appearance of the woman called Caroline and her husband is to give the reader a glimpse of how Scrooge behaves to his debtors, refusing to give them even a week to pay off their arrears, even though it might land them in a debtor's prison.

The two charity collectors do not even have names; they are merely representatives of the type of better-off people in society who feel it is their duty to help those less fortunate. They give up their time at Christmas to go round to offices and persuade businessmen to subscribe a sum of money to help the poor. They stand for the kind of goodwill that Dickens considered to be the main part of Christmas and they are examples of how he thought well-off people should behave. They cannot believe that Scrooge would reject the opportunity and when he mentions workhouses and prisons, they point out, **"Under the impression that they scarcely furnish Christian cheer of mind or body to the multitude,"** returned the gentleman, **"a few of us are endeavouring to raise a fund to buy the Poor some meat and drink, and means of warmth. We choose this time, because it is a time, of all others, when Want is keenly felt, and Abundance rejoices. What shall I put you down for?"** *(Stave 1).* It is symbolic that one of the first people Scrooge meets after his conversion is one of these men, who is overjoyed at the huge sum he is offered for, as Scrooge tells him, **"A great many back-payments are included in it, I assure you"** *(Stave 5).*

The two anonymous boys mentioned at the beginning and end of the story are treated in very different ways and their role is to show the contrast in Scrooge's attitude towards children. The first is the young carol singer who is driven away. The second boy meets with a very different reception as Scrooge calls him **"intelligent"** and **"delightful'**, and offers him money to run an errand. The reader may assume that Scrooge's experiences of the Cratchit family on his time travels might have something to do with this.

The final set of minor characters who are shown in detail in the story are those seen by Scrooge in Stave 4 selling the hangings off the bed and the clothes off the corpse, which he later realizes is his own. These unattractive people are what the Victorians would consider 'the undeserving poor'. Instead of feeling pity for the man who died alone and friendless, they take advantage of his lonely state to steal everything possible. Their total lack of humanity and charity is shown in their comment, **"This is the end of it, you see! He frightened every one away from him when he was alive, to profit us when he was dead! Ha, ha, ha!"** *(Stave 4).* While it is hard to feel sympathy for Scrooge, we can only regard such people with horror. Dickens was well aware that not all the poor were like those on whom the Ghost of Christmas Present sprinkles goodwill. Their role in the story is to warn Scrooge, and others who behave like him, what may happen if they drive others away from them and have nobody even to mourn for them at the end.

Activity 11

1. With a partner, look at each of the minor characters. Answer the following questions:

   - What does the reader learn about them?
   - What is their role in the story? Why does Dickens include them?

   Find evidence from the text to support your views.

2. Look at Fezziwig's party scene in Stave 2 and Fred's party scene in Stave 3. These scenes are full of what is called 'cameos' – characters who appear briefly. Choose two such characters from each scene and discuss what the reader is told about them and why you think Dickens gives this information.

Writing about characters

Upgrade

You may be asked to answer a question about a character or a group of characters from the novella. You will need to show your knowledge of them not just as a person, but as a created character with a specific role or function in the story. You will need to cover the following in your answer:

- the kind of things the author gives the character to say and how they say them
- the kind of things the author gives the character to do and how they do them
- what the author makes the narrator tell us about the character
- how the author makes other characters react to them
- why the author has included this character in the novella (their role or function).

You will need to give detailed evidence from the novella to support all the points you make, including quotations where appropriate.

Character map

Scrooge's business associates

Other members of the Cratchit family

Scrooge's personal associates

Ghosts and spirits

Others who deal with Scrooge

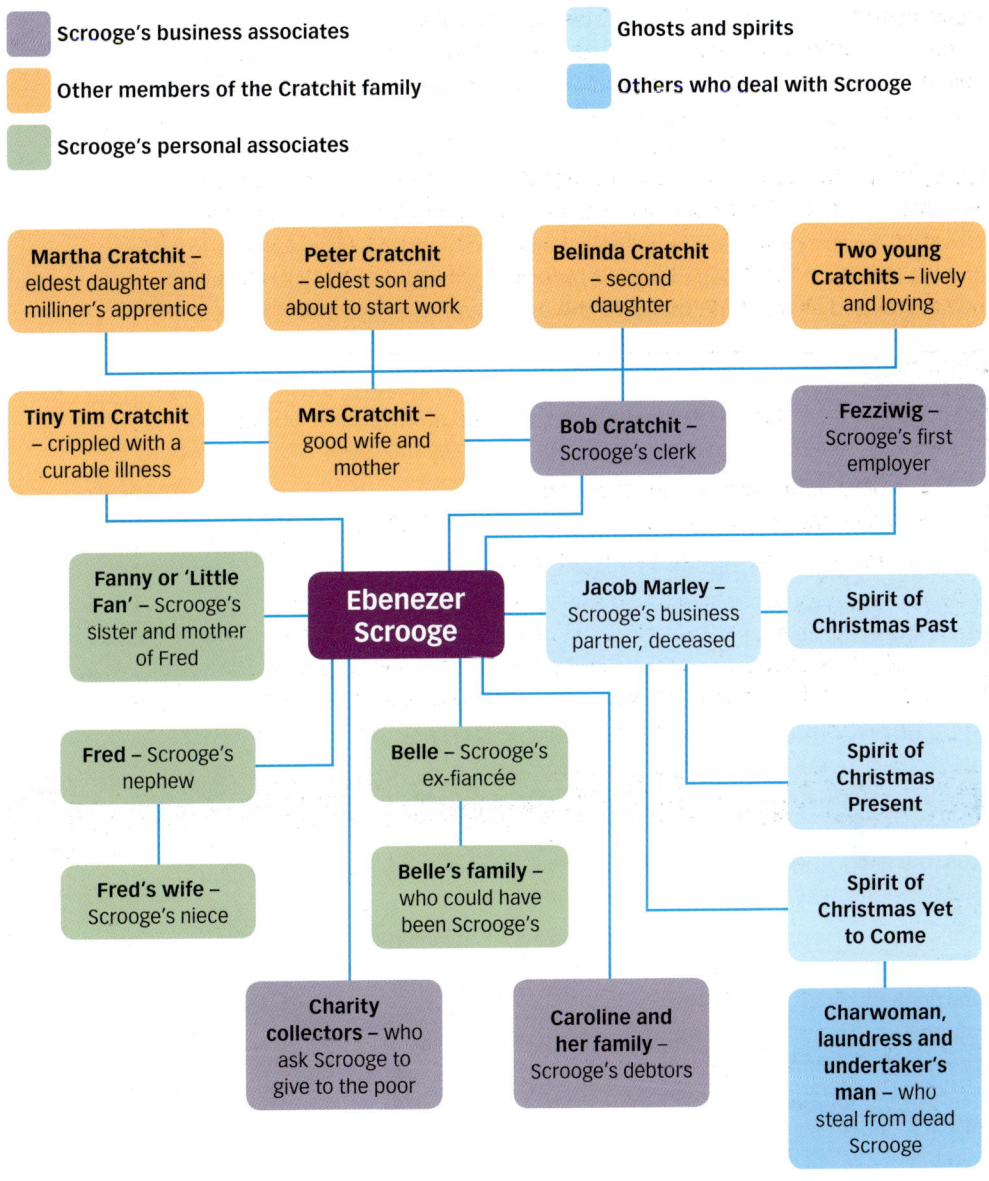

Martha Cratchit – eldest daughter and milliner's apprentice

Peter Cratchit – eldest son and about to start work

Belinda Cratchit – second daughter

Two young Cratchits – lively and loving

Tiny Tim Cratchit – crippled with a curable illness

Mrs Cratchit – good wife and mother

Bob Cratchit – Scrooge's clerk

Fezziwig – Scrooge's first employer

Fanny or 'Little Fan' – Scrooge's sister and mother of Fred

Ebenezer Scrooge

Jacob Marley – Scrooge's business partner, deceased

Spirit of Christmas Past

Fred – Scrooge's nephew

Belle – Scrooge's ex-fiancée

Spirit of Christmas Present

Fred's wife – Scrooge's niece

Belle's family – who could have been Scrooge's

Spirit of Christmas Yet to Come

Charity collectors – who ask Scrooge to give to the poor

Caroline and her family – Scrooge's debtors

Charwoman, laundress and undertaker's man – who steal from dead Scrooge

Dickens's writing is noted for its vivid description and memorable characters. His stories are rich in detail and description although he can also write tense action sequences and pinpoint a place or person in a few well-chosen words. More than anything else he is a dramatic writer (he used to perform his works in public), which can make parts of his novels appear either sentimental or melodramatic.

Humour

Dickens's humour is one of his most effective techniques. It takes various forms, including wordplay and puns, **hyperbole**, humorous comparisons, digression, irony and the use of vivid **phrases** to provide an amusing image, like the young Cratchits being 'steeped in sage and onion to the eyebrows' *(Stave 3)*, which tells us how the children had stuffing all over their faces.

Dickens is fond of wordplay and puns, and he shows this even in the preface, where his hope that the story may 'haunt their houses pleasantly' plays on the idea of 'haunt' as something ghosts do, as well as something that stays with you. This immediately indicates to the reader that the tale, although billed as 'A Ghost Story', is not meant to be scary. Later, in an 'aside' to the reader about Scrooge's clerk, he remarks 'Bob had but fifteen "Bob" a-week himself' *(Stave 3)*, a pun on Bob's name and the slang term for a shilling, as well as a reference to the clerk's low wage. The punning also extends to the supernatural happenings that begin on Christmas Eve with Scrooge's comment to his erstwhile partner, "There's more of gravy than of grave about you, whatever you are!" *(Stave 1)*. This refers to his previous comment that the apparition is the result of undigested beef, a meat usually eaten with gravy, but playing on the idea of ghosts rising from the grave. The humorous comments that Dickens gives Scrooge here show his attempts to cover up his fear.

Marley's face appears on Scrooge's door knocker

When Dickens wants to reveal the underlying comic elements of the narrative, one of his methods is to pile **qualifiers** one upon the other, as when he describes Scrooge as 'a squeezing, wrenching, grasping, scraping, clutching, covetous, old sinner!' *(Stave 1)*. Because he has been excessive in the number of descriptors used, the impression of evil is undermined, especially when he concludes with 'old sinner', which has a suggestion of familiarity about it. It has the effect of presenting Scrooge as less wicked than his words and actions imply, thus preparing the reader for his reformation. This hyperbole is also used for comic effect when Dickens describes the Christmas shoppers who 'tumbled up against each other at the door, crashing their wicker baskets wildly, and left their purchases upon the counter, and came running back to fetch them, and committed hundreds of the like mistakes, in the best humour possible' *(Stave 3).* Dickens is using a number of actions piled one after the other to create a scene of happy chaos. It is intended to amuse the reader by its familiarity as well as showing it as part of the Christmas spirit.

Dickens uses comedy in some of his comparisons, for example, when he comments, 'Old Marley was as dead as a door-nail' *(Stave 1).* This signals to the reader that Marley's death is not something to be taken seriously, especially as it is followed by a digression on the **simile** itself, and instantly highlights the dark comic undertone that runs throughout the novella. These 'asides' to the reader generally serve to lower the tension and are intended to amuse because they are discussing such trivial points. They create a familiarity with the reader, as if they were chatting to a friend.

Dickens's humour can also be ironic at times. For instance, at the beginning of Stave 3 we are told, 'Now, being prepared for almost anything, he was not by any means prepared for nothing; and, consequently, when the Bell struck One, and no shape appeared, he was taken with a violent fit of trembling'. Dickens uses **bathos** for effect here. Scrooge has mentally prepared himself for any kind of supernatural happening, so when nothing happens it frightens him.

Activity 1

1. Find examples of each the following language features in the novella:
   - wordplay and puns
   - hyperbole
   - humorous comparisons
   - irony.

2. Write one or two paragraphs about Dickens's use of the above techniques. Consider the effects of this type of humour. Why do you think Dickens chose to include it in his 'Ghost Story'?

3. Compare your answers with another student. Do you agree or disagree with their comments about Dickens's use of humour in *A Christmas Carol*? Why?

bathos an abrupt change from extraordinary to everyday, giving a comic effect

hyperbole exaggeration for the purpose of emphasis

phrase a group of words in a sentence that could not form a sentence on their own

qualifiers describing words such as adjectives (which describe nouns) and adverbs (which describe verbs)

simile a comparison that shows it is comparing by using 'like' or 'as', e.g. 'solitary as an oyster'

Satire

As a writer and performer, Dickens was well aware that preaching at people about mending their ways would not be effective, whereas if you entertained them they would first be amused and then start to think about what they'd read. *A Christmas Carol* is a good example of this technique and has been popular for over 150 years as a result. Dickens is a **satirical** writer because he tries to influence his readers towards reforming society and individuals. He targets attitudes to poverty, to education, to religion and to common ideas about childhood and social responsibility.

The main target in this story is, of course, Ebenezer Scrooge, who is larger than life but whose behaviour illustrates attitudes held by many wealthy people in Victorian England. After telling us that Scrooge was the only person involved in Marley's funeral, the narrator comments, **'And even Scrooge was not so dreadfully cut up by the sad event, but that he was an excellent man of business on the very day of the funeral, and solemnised it with an undoubted bargain'** *(Stave 1).* This amuses, but also gives the reader a very good idea of the kind of man he is, who would conduct business and drive hard bargains on the very day of his only friend's funeral. Dickens is using satire to make the reader aware of Scrooge's moral failure and, by extension, to highlight what he saw as the moral failure of some of the wealthy in Victorian society.

Dickens also uses satire to criticize the widespread belief in the ideas of economist Thomas Malthus, who spread the notion that an increase in population would lead to scarce resources and starvation. This is reflected by Scrooge when he comments, **"If they would rather die... they had better do it, and decrease the surplus population"** *(Stave 1).* Dickens intends this comment to shock his readers into hoping that Scrooge does not mean what he says. Dickens uses these words again when Scrooge expresses an interest in Tiny Tim, making him feel guilty and sorry for them when he sees his words applied to real people.

Dickens is also saying that this was a good excuse for the rich to make sure they had more than their share of those resources. The grasping nature of Scrooge's city acquaintances is shown in

Teaching girls to read in a Ragged School in London, 1868

Stave 4, after his death: **"I don't mind going if a lunch is provided," observed the gentleman with the excrescence on his nose. "But I must be fed, if I make one"** *(Stave 4)*. Dickens is showing that Scrooge is not the only person with a mean and grasping nature, as his acquaintances will only attend his funeral if they are offered something in return. This is intended to expose the nature of a 'friendship' built only on money.

However, Dickens does not reserve his satire entirely for the better-off members of society. The mercenary and uncharitable commerce we are shown between those given the care of Scrooge's body shows an equally reprehensible attitude among some of the poor, especially the pretended generosity of 'Joe' in his filthy hovel: **"I always give too much to ladies. It's a weakness of mine, and that's the way I ruin myself"** *(Stave 4)*. The reader knows that this is mere hypocrisy and the fence is paying far less than the goods are worth. Dickens is using satirical humour to show the man for what he is. Thus the moral failings of society are spread throughout. We may also suspect that, in common with Scrooge, Joe could afford to live in nicer surroundings but chooses not to.

Satire often works through the use of irony, which may or may not be humorous. There are different kinds of irony: <mark>verbal irony</mark>, <mark>situational irony</mark> and <mark>dramatic irony</mark>.

Activity 2

1. Look at the ironic examples below and identify which type of irony each represents. Discuss your choice with a partner and write a sentence about what Dickens is suggesting.
   - "You're quite a powerful speaker, sir... I wonder you don't go into Parliament." *(Stave 1, to Fred)*
   - 'The clerk... poked the fire, and extinguished the last frail spark for ever.' *(Stave 1)*
   - In Stave 4, when the reader knows the dead man is Scrooge himself, although Scrooge doesn't realize it until he sees his name on the gravestone.

   Which examples would you describe as amusing and which as serious?
2. Find one other example of satire and one other example of irony, and make a note of them.
3. Write two or three paragraphs about Dickens's use of satire and irony, both humorous and serious, and how he exposes the failings of Scrooge and Victorian society in general.

---

dramatic irony when an audience or reader knows something the characters do not, e.g. when the audience in *Romeo and Juliet* knows that Juliet isn't really dead, but Romeo does not

satire exposing the failings of people or societies by making fun of them

situational irony when the outcome of a situation is the reverse of that intended, e.g. someone being caught in a trap they laid for another person

verbal irony words that say the opposite of what someone actually means, e.g. 'What a lovely day!' when it is raining

Parable, allegory, fairy tale and symbolism

A Christmas Carol is a story that works on several levels of meaning. It is a **parable** because it has a moral lesson; it is an **allegory** because it uses figures that represent abstract ideas; it is a fairy tale as it has elements of the supernatural and tells of good against evil; and it uses many symbols to reinforce its ideas.

The story itself is a parable of redemption, a moral lesson for the selfish and avaricious within an entertaining tale of ghosts and Christmas. Within the story, goodness is bound up with a generous enjoyment of giving, both material and, more importantly, emotional. Evil is shown, not merely through Scrooge's miserly refusal to give, but through his refusal of human contact. Even his colleagues in the city barely know him. He seems to hate himself as much as he hates anything else and his whole life is spent in the acquisition of wealth that brings him no pleasure. It is this that makes his nephew and his clerk feel sorry for him.

The parable also works through symbolism, particularly in its contrasts. Fog is one of them, obscuring the clear moral view of the protagonist. Almost the first thing we read about Scrooge's location is, **'The fog came pouring in at every chink and keyhole, and was so dense without, that although the court was of the narrowest, the houses opposite were mere phantoms'** *(Stave 1)*. This use of **pathetic fallacy** signifies the fog of ignorance and prejudice that clouds Scrooge's brain and emotions. In sharp contrast, when he is a reformed man, the weather changes: **'No fog, no mist; clear, bright, jovial, stirring, cold; cold, piping for the blood to dance to; Golden sunlight; Heavenly sky; sweet fresh air'** *(Stave 5)*. Now he can see clearly what is really important. In the same way, the cold that used to come from his frozen emotions and cold spirit is now one that sets the blood singing and brings him alive.

allegory a story with a second meaning behind the obvious one, using abstract ideas as personified characters

parable a story related to people's own experiences that illustrates a moral lesson, often through personification and/or metaphor

pathetic fallacy the idea that nature reflects human feelings

There are other symbols that are important to the story. Jacob Marley's chain is, he tells Scrooge, one that he made for himself. This chain is made, not of links, but **'of cash-boxes, keys, padlocks, ledgers, deeds, and heavy purses wrought in steel'** *(Stave 1)* – in other words, of all the financial dealings that Marley thought were so important during his life, but which now prevent him from finding peace after death.

Marley's Ghost tells Scrooge that his behaviour in life now acts as the heavy chain he must carry in death

The allegorical aspect of the story can be seen in the ghosts, who represent memory (the past), good example (the present) and fear of death (the future), as well as the figures of Ignorance and Want who threaten the social order. The actual story, after the introduction of the dead Marley and Scrooge himself, begins **'Once upon a time…'** *(Stave 1),* which signals a fairy tale, traditionally a story of evil being overcome by good and in which supernatural events can be taken for granted.

There are *three* spirits, a religious and magic number often used in fairy tales and myths (for example, three bears, three wise men, three wishes, etc.). Other symbols include the light of memory that shines from the Ghost of Christmas Past and reminds Scrooge of his childhood and youth, a light that he tries to suppress. The horn of plenty carried by the Ghost of Christmas Present is another, showing by example how a sprinkle of generous giving can enrich lives. The silence of the Ghost of Christmas Yet To Come shows how the future cannot speak to us, but may reveal what will happen if we continue in the same pattern to the one inevitable end, represented by the gravestone.

Activity 3

In a small group, discuss the ways in which *A Christmas Carol* can be considered an allegory or a parable.

Why do you think Dickens might have chosen to use these forms to present his ideas?

Would the novella have had the same effect if Dickens had written a social commentary about the divisions between rich and poor in his society? Why or why not?

Tension and suspense

Dickens is well aware of the power that suspense has in a ghost story. He shows it in *The Signalman* among others, but in *A Christmas Carol*, although he uses the **gothic** elements of spectres and the supernatural, he often undercuts the suspense with humour, to show that the story is light-hearted rather than blood-chilling.

Dickens builds up to the appearance of Marley's Ghost in stages. First, he depicts Scrooge seeing Marley's face in the door knocker, followed by the vision of the ghostly hearse going up the stairs in front of him. He tells of Scrooge checking his apartment thoroughly, even the wardrobes and under the bed. This suggests Scrooge's nervousness, while being amusing at the same time because of the repetition of 'nobody' and the idea of the dressing gown in a **'suspicious attitude'** *(Stave 1)*. He then progresses to Ebenezer's walking restlessly and follows this with his seeing the disused bell: **'It was with great astonishment, and with a strange, inexplicable dread, that as he looked, he saw this bell begin to swing'** *(Stave 1)*. As the bells stop ringing and silence descends, he hears another, more ominous sound: **'a clanking noise, deep down below; as if some person were dragging a heavy chain over the casks in the wine merchant's cellar'** *(Stave 1)*. This is succeeded by the sound of the cellar door flying open and then **'he heard the noise much louder, on the floors below; then coming up the stairs; then coming straight towards his door'** *(Stave 1)*. Dickens then uses bathos to dispel the tension created by this succession of events, by describing the Ghost looking much as it had in life and with the humorous exchanges between it and Scrooge.

There is a feeling of suspense throughout the story as we wonder what each of the spirits will be like and whether Scrooge will repent. Later, there is the question of whether Tiny Tim will live and what will happen to the Cratchits if Bob loses his job. In Stave 4, in an example of dramatic irony, there is added tension as the reader waits for Scrooge to make the connection between the dead man he sees and himself. Dickens keeps us waiting until near the end of the chapter, creating suspense through the description of the graveyard and the dialogue with the Ghost until **'Scrooge crept towards it, trembling as he went; and following the finger, read upon the stone of the neglected grave his own name, EBENEZER SCROOGE'** *(Stave 4)*. In this sentence alone, Dickens's skill in building tension is evident. The revelation (**'his own name, EBENEZER SCROOGE'**) is carefully positioned at the end of the sentence, preceded by a sequence of clauses that describe Scrooge's tentative movements towards the grave.

> **gothic** a term used to describe stories or poems with a horror or supernatural theme

Activity 4

With a partner, look at the end of Stave 3 from 'The chimes were ringing the three quarters past eleven at that moment' to the end.

a) Make notes on the way Dickens uses language to build tension in this episode. You should consider:

- what Scrooge first notices under the Ghost's robe
- the adjectives Dickens uses to describe the children when they first appear
- the actions he gives the children
- Dickens's use of sentence structures to add tension
- the way he describes them that makes them sound inhuman
- Scrooge's reaction to them
- the words the Ghost uses about them and the warning it gives
- how it turns Scrooge's own words back on him.

b) Write two or three paragraphs on how Dickens creates tension in this scene and its effect.

Figurative language

Dickens makes use of much **figurative language** in his writing. He uses personification frequently, for example, as in this rather fanciful description of Scrooge's apartment looking out of place and imagining **'it must have run there when it was a young house, playing at hide-and-seek with other houses, and forgotten the way out again'** (Stave 1). He also uses many comparisons, often for comic effect as when Scrooge, delighted at his new self, exclaims, **"I am as light as a feather, I am as happy as an angel, I am as merry as a schoolboy. I am as giddy as a drunken man"** (Stave 5). His metaphors are equally abundant, although not always so amusing. When he says of Scrooge, **'The cold within him froze his old features'** (Stave 1), the reader knows that this is an emotional and spiritual cold and not just the winter weather.

Scrooge becomes a good friend to Bob Cratchit and his family

> **figurative language** language that uses 'figures of speech' such as metaphors, similes, personification, repetition, hyperbole, bathos, etc.

When Dickens uses repetition, which he often does, it is to emphasize something; for instance, when Scrooge becomes **'as good a friend, as good a master, and as good a man, as the good old city knew, or any other good old city, town, or borough, in the good old world'** *(Stave 5).*

Speech patterns

Dickens cleverly presents the differences in his characters through their unique patterns of speech or **idiolect**. Scrooge's manner of talking is short, terse and economical, which fits the mean-spirited nature of his character. He appears to regard overly descriptive or metaphorical language as kind of extravagance and dismisses Fred's heartfelt defence of the spirit of Christmas with a curt **"Good afternoon!"** *(Stave 1).* At the beginning of the novella, Scrooge's speech is characterized by short, declarative statements or questions: **"Merry Christmas! What right have you to be merry? What reason have you to be merry? You're poor enough"** *(Stave 1).* However, Scrooge's redemption at the end of the novella is reflected in a change in his use of language. Following his transformation, his speech is littered with exclamations, suggestive of a newfound joy in both life and language: **"Oh Jacob Marley! Heaven, and the Christmas Time be praised for this! I say it on my knees, old Jacob, on my knees!"** *(Stave 5).*

Marley's language is characterized by **elevated diction**, which seems fitting for a creature from another dimension: **"Oh! captive, bound and double-ironed... not to know, that ages of incessant labour, by immortal creatures, for this earth must pass into eternity before the good of which it is susceptible is all developed"** *(Stave 1).* His speech is also similarly marked by repetition: **"Yet such was I Oh! such was I!'** *(Stave 1)* and **"Mankind was my business. The common welfare was my business; charity, forbearance, and benevolence, were, all, my business"** *(Stave 1).* This repetition mirrors Marley's punishment itself: he is bound to repeatedly wander the Earth, caught in a cycle where he is forced to witness the suffering of mankind that he was so blind to during his life.

> ### Activity 5
>
> Select another character from the novella, for example, Bob Cratchit, Fred or one of the spirits, and make notes on their speech patterns. Consider:
>
> - the types of words that they use
> - their use of sentence structures
> - their use of figurative language.
>
> What does their language use tell you about their character?

elevated diction 'high' or complex forms of speech, using precise words and a formal style

idiolect an individual's unique speech pattern

Dickens presents his characters partly through their diction and partly through their vocabulary. Those like Fred and the Cratchits use endearments and words and phrases that suggest kindness and good cheer. The spirits and ghosts use words and phrases that suggest doom or warning, and, occasionally, approval. Scrooge's own words and phrases change as the story progresses, from his dismissal of Christmas and refusal to give money, through expressions of regret and interest in those he is shown, to happy generosity at the end.

Activity 6

Pair each quotation below with the correct character.

A "Let me leave it alone, then" *(Stave 1)*

B "A small matter... to make these silly folks so full of gratitude." *(Stave 2)*

C "Will you decide what men shall live, what men shall die?" *(Stave 3)*

D "He has given us plenty of merriment, I am sure" *(Stave 3)*

E "Every person has a right to take care of themselves." *(Stave 4)*

F "It would have done you good to see how green a place it is." *(Stave 4)*

G "What a delightful boy!" *(Stave 5)*

1 Ghost of Christmas Present

2 Scrooge (after the spirits)

3 Charwoman

4 Scrooge (before the spirits)

5 Bob Cratchit

6 Ghost of Christmas Past

7 Fred

Compare your answers with other students'. What features helped you to decide?

Writing about language

Upgrade

Examiners are often disappointed that students do not write in enough detail about an author's use of language. It is very important, whatever you are asked to focus on in your exam question, that you include discussion of a writer's style and techniques in some depth, supported by references to and short quotations from the text. For example, it is not enough to comment on satire in the novella. You need to show how Dickens has chosen to use satire for specific purposes. You should comment in detail, using short examples.

Poverty and wealth

Dickens wrote his novels with the idea not only of entertaining his readers but of making them think about social attitudes and **morality**. He was very clear about the evils of poverty and, in particular, the lack of education that helped to perpetuate it. He saw the divisions between rich and poor, and the evils to which this led, as wrong in a society that claimed to be Christian. He shows this in *A Christmas Carol* through the distinctions he makes between those like Scrooge and Marley, who are only interested in making money, and those like Fred and the charity collectors, who go out of their way to help others.

> **morality** a set of principles and values, concerning what is right and wrong

Scrooge represents one end of the scale between wealth and poverty: **"I don't make merry myself at Christmas and I can't afford to make idle people merry. I help to support the establishments I have mentioned – they cost enough; and those who are badly off must go there"** *(Stave 1)*. It is apparent that Scrooge must be rich for his word is always taken in the city, which is where he does business. What he does with his money is a mystery, for he leads a frugal life and, as Fred points out, **"His wealth is of no use to him. He don't do any good with it. He don't make himself comfortable with it"** *(Stave 3)*. His only satisfaction seems to be in accumulating money and in thwarting the good intentions of others, like the charity collectors and his nephew.

Much further down the social scale is the family of his clerk, Bob Cratchit. They are not destitute by any means, but nobody could call them other than poor: **'They were not a handsome family; they were not well dressed; their shoes were far from being water-proof; their clothes were scanty; and Peter might have known, and very likely did, the inside of a pawnbroker's'** *(Stave 3)*. It would take little effort on Scrooge's part to change their lives and, in the course of the night, he realizes this. Meanwhile, they do not complain about their lot, making the most of what they have, as we see from Mrs Cratchit in her **'twice-turned gown'** *(Stave 3)*, which she has cheered up with some cheap ribbon.

At the very bottom of society are those whom Scrooge consigns to the workhouses and prisons, represented by the childish figures of Ignorance and Want at the end of Stave 3: **"They are Man's," said the Spirit, looking down upon them, "And they cling to me, appealing from their fathers. This boy is Ignorance. This girl is Want. Beware them both, and all of their degree, but most of all beware this boy, for on his brow I see that written which is Doom, unless the writing be erased."** Dickens's message is clear and unambiguous: if the children of the poor are left uneducated, it will be the worse for society. This is further illustrated by the scene in Stave 4 where the goods stolen from the dead man are sold in a place described as a **'den of infamous resort, [where] there was a low-browed,** beetling shop, below a pent-house roof, where iron, old rags, bottles, bones, and greasy offal, were bought. Upon the floor within, were piled up heaps of rusty keys, nails, chains, hinges, files, scales, weights, and refuse iron of all kinds. Secrets that few would like to scrutinise were bred and hidden in mountains of unseemly rags, masses of corrupted fat, and sepulchres of bones'. Dickens's use of accumulated images here gives the reader a feeling of revulsion, which is extended to the people who live in or visit it. Dickens shows this kind of slum to be the breeding ground of crime and corruption, and the two children are products of it. They are also the products of the uncaring attitude of wealthy businessmen like Scrooge, as Dickens points out.

The Ghost of Christmas Present with the children Ignorance and Want

> **Key quotations**
>
> "If they would rather die," said Scrooge, "they had better do it, and decrease the surplus population." *(Stave 1)*

Activity 1

1. Find three examples from the novella to show:
   - how well-off people celebrated Christmas
   - how poor people celebrated Christmas.
2. Explain what your examples show about the divisions in Victorian society. Write a brief paragraph, outlining why Dickens wanted to show the contrast.

Greed and generosity

Dickens makes a clear distinction between the wealth created by money and the richness that comes from the spirit and the emotions. Scrooge has more money than he knows what to do with, but his spirit is so mean that he does not even make himself comfortable, never mind anyone else. This shows itself in the reaction of others: 'Nobody ever stopped him in the street to say, with gladsome looks, "My dear Scrooge, how are you? When will you come to see me?"' *(Stave 1)*.

His refusal to attend his nephew's Christmas party has nothing to do with money – it might even save him some – and everything to do with his inability to give of himself.

In contrast to this, his nephew Fred refuses to be defeated and says he will ask him every year in spite of his curmudgeonly treatment. He is genuinely pleased when his uncle does turn up. His party is given out of a generous desire to see everyone come together at Christmas in the spirit of the season and is reflected in all sections of society, as the Ghost of Christmas Present reveals to Scrooge, even in a distant lighthouse and on a boat out at sea. This emotional giving is true also of the Cratchits, who have so little materially, but who are rich in love and cheerfulness: **'Everybody had something to say about it, but nobody said or thought it was at all a small pudding for a large family. It would have been flat heresy to do so. Any Cratchit would have blushed to hint at such a thing'** *(Stave 3).*

During his journey with the second spirit, Scrooge confuses the true message of Christmas shown by this personification of generosity, with those evangelical churchgoers who want to close everything down on Sundays. This includes the bakers, who are allowed to open their ovens for the poor to cook their roast dinners: **"There are some upon this earth of yours," returned the Spirit, "who lay claim to know us, and who do their deeds of passion, pride, ill-will, hatred, envy, bigotry, and selfishness in our name, who are as strange to us and all our kith and kin, as if they had never lived. Remember that, and charge their doings on themselves, not us"** *(Stave 3).* Dickens himself was a liberal Christian who wanted to propagate the message of love, goodwill and peace. He disliked the hypocritical attitudes of many upper and middle-class Christians, who thought it was dangerous to educate the poor and wanted to stop their Sunday pastimes.

> **Key quotations**
>
> **The Lord Mayor, in the stronghold of the mighty Mansion House, gave orders to his fifty cooks and butlers to keep Christmas as a Lord Mayor's household should; and even the little tailor, whom he had fined five shillings on the previous Monday for being drunk and bloodthirsty in the streets, stirred up tomorrow's pudding in his garret, while his lean wife and the baby sallied out to buy the beef.** *(Stave 1)*

Activity 2

Create a short presentation about the theme of 'Greed and generosity' in *A Christmas Carol*. Your presentation should include the following:

- a discussion of the theme and its importance in the novella
- quotations and examples from the text to illustrate points in your discussion.

Present your ideas to the class. Take feedback from your classmates about what they think you covered well and what you could improve on.

Time and space

The theme of time is very important to this story. Scrooge is no longer young and his business partner is already dead, so he cannot afford to wait too long if he is to reform his ways. In a sense, the story is about time travel, as the ghostly visitations disrupt time altogether. Past, present and future all come together in a single night. Time is frequently mentioned, as when Scrooge checks it is time to leave the office or that it is exactly seven years since Marley's death. The fact that time is playing tricks on him is an indication that something strange is about to happen. The Scrooge who is strict with Bob Cratchit about punctuality finds that time has no meaning through that night.

Wintertime already seems too short, as we read, **'The city clocks had only just gone three, but it was quite dark already – it had not been light all day – and candles were flaring in the windows of the neighbouring offices, like ruddy smears upon the palpable brown air'** *(Stave 1)*. At the outset of the novella, there is already some confusion of day and night because of the darkness brought by the fog.

When Marley's Ghost appears, there is further unravelling of the idea of time. The Ghost claims that, over the course of the seven years, he has been travelling all the time, with **"No rest, no peace. Incessant torture of remorse"** *(Stave 1)*. This marks a discrepancy between the human understanding of time, through man-made clocks, and eternal time, which is measured only in terms of torment.

Before the first visitation Scrooge is surprised by the sudden disruption to time: **'To his great astonishment the heavy bell went on from six to seven, and from seven to eight, and regularly up to twelve; then stopped. Twelve! It was past two when he went to bed. The clock was wrong. An icicle must have got into the works. Twelve!'** *(Stave 2)*. Each spirit visits him on the stroke of one and Scrooge is expecting, following what Marley has told him, that they will visit over three successive nights. However the spirits are not bound by time or space and they manage to cram most of Scrooge's life and future into a single stretch.

The Ghost of Christmas Past has power over space, as well as over time. In Stave 2 he seems hardly able to move and yet, **'As the words were spoken, they passed through the wall, and stood upon an open country road, with fields on either hand'**. This is almost like the curtain going up on a play and shortly afterwards Dickens describes how, when the Ghost talks of another Christmas, **'Scrooge's former self grew larger at the words, and the room became a little darker and more dirty. The panels shrunk, the windows cracked; fragments of plaster fell out of the ceiling, and the naked laths were shown instead; but how all this was brought about, Scrooge knew no more than you do'** *(Stave 2)*.

When Scrooge is taken across the globe by the Ghost of Christmas Present in Stave 3, we are told **'Much they saw, and far they went, and many homes they visited, but always with a happy end'**. Scrooge himself finds this amazing, as the narrator remarks, **'It was a long night, if it were only a night; but Scrooge had**

his doubts of this, because the Christmas Holidays appeared to be condensed into the space of time they passed together' *(Stave 3).* The Ghost is able to go wherever it wishes and see whatever it likes while remaining invisible and inaudible – as does Scrooge while he is with it, for we are told that during the games at Fred's party, **'forgetting in the interest he had in what was going on, that his voice made no sound in their ears, he sometimes came out with his guess quite loud'** *(Stave 3).*

Of course, Scrooge recognizes only his past and his present, not his future – until he sees his own name on the gravestone and realizes his time has run out. He then becomes desperate to know if the Ghost has shown him what *must* be or whether he can alter it. His relief when he finds it is morning shows in the following, **'YES! and the bedpost was his own. The bed was his own, the room was his own. Best and happiest of all, the Time before him was his own, to make amends in!'** *(Stave 5).* The value of time means something quite different to him than when he said of his business that it **"occupies me constantly"** *(Stave 1).* He now realizes that time has been measured differently by his supernatural visitors: **"It's Christmas Day!" said Scrooge to himself. "I haven't missed it. The Spirits have done it all in one night. They can do anything they like. Of course they can. Of course they can"** *(Stave 5).*

Christmas at Fred's is full of generosity and fun, which reaps its own rewards

Time is shown to be bound up with the opportunity either to do good or to fail in that duty. Marley's Ghost makes that plain at the start and Scrooge's happiness at the end is a result of the fact that he has time to make amends. Scrooge's journey with the three spirits seems to be a physical one, although it defies the normal conventions of time and space, but it is also a metaphorical journey through his life, and reveals to Scrooge all his past errors and failings. The feelings that the journey creates in Scrooge result in his change of heart and his conversion into a benevolent and cheerful man.

> **Key quotations**
>
> **"Not to know that any Christian spirit working kindly in its little sphere, whatever it may be, will find its mortal life too short for its vast means of usefulness. Not to know that no space of regret can make amends for one life's opportunity misused!"** *(Stave 1)*

Activity 3

1. Divide a piece of paper into three columns headed 'Past', 'Present' and 'Future'. Under each heading make a list of the places and events that take place with each of the three spirits on the night of Christmas Eve.

2. Divide another piece of paper into two columns. Head the first column 'Physical journey' and the second 'Metaphorical journey'. In the first column, list the events that occur over the course of the night (in the past, present and future). In the second column, make a note of how each event affects Scrooge and begins to change him as a person. An example has been done for you below.

Physical journey	Metaphorical journey
The first spirit takes to Scrooge to his old school.	Scrooge remembers his loneliness and sobs – the first sign of his feelings.

Light and dark

The antithesis between light and dark, and the warmth and cold associated with them, are used throughout the story to represent the differences between good and evil, generosity and greed. Pathetic fallacy is used by Dickens to present the change in Scrooge: at the beginning of the story the day is dark and the fog obscures everything; by the end of the story it is **'Golden sunlight'** *(Stave 5)*.

At the start of the story, in Stave 1, Scrooge is described as emotionally and spiritually frozen: **'A frosty rime was on his head, and on his eyebrows, and his wiry chin. He carried his own low temperature always about with him; he iced his office in the dog-days; and didn't thaw it one degree at Christmas'**. His opposite here is his nephew Fred who **'had so heated himself with rapid walking in the fog and frost, this nephew of Scrooge's, that he was all in a glow; his face was ruddy and handsome; his eyes sparkled, and his breath smoked again'** *(Stave 1)*. Here is a man who is totally alive and glowing with emotional and spiritual generosity. Having failed to thaw his rigid uncle, **'He stopped at the outer door to bestow the greetings of the season on the clerk, who, cold as he was, was warmer than Scrooge; for he returned them cordially'** *(Stave 1)*. Outside, the cold is intense but workmen have lit a brazier and are warming themselves, while the brightness of the shops forms a contrast to the gloom and fog.

The darkness of Scrooge's apartments is described as being more than half a dozen street lamps could dispel, but the miser doesn't care: **'Darkness is cheap, and Scrooge liked it'** *(Stave 1)*. He is a creature of the dark and thus leans towards evil rather than good. In a sense, he is out in the dark of his own free will, staying solitary and exchanging greetings with none but those whose financial dealings he admires. As a child, this loneliness was forced on him by his father's attitude, which left him solitary at Christmas in school. This is opposed to his experience as Fezziwig's apprentice, where Christmas was a time of light and warmth and people gathering to enjoy themselves, and none left out. Despite this example, Scrooge has made an idol of money and has thus become part of the dark and the cold. The story of the novella is how he comes into the light and warmth of good fellowship and kindness.

The Ghost of Christmas Past has its own light: the light of memory that illuminates past events and actions. Scrooge's first act is to try and snuff it: **'Perhaps Scrooge could not have told anybody why, if anybody could have asked him; but he had a special desire to see the Spirit in his cap; and begged him to be covered'** *(Stave 2)*. He doesn't want to be reminded of the past, but without the memory of what was, it is impossible to progress. The seeds of the solitary miser can be found in the lonely child and Scrooge sobs as he recalls his situation. Both this Ghost and the Ghost of Christmas Present show Scrooge the illumination and glow that pervade the places where people, especially families, come together in happiness, whatever their material circumstances may be. He watches from the outside, even trying to join in as his frozen nature thaws. By the end, he is sending Bob Cratchit for more coal: **"Make up the fires, and buy another coal-scuttle before you dot another i, Bob Cratchit!"** *(Stave 5)*.

Key quotations

By this time it was getting dark, and snowing pretty heavily; and as Scrooge and the Spirit went along the streets, the brightness of the roaring fires in kitchens, parlours, and all sorts of rooms, was wonderful. Here, the flickering of the blaze showed preparations for a cosy dinner, with hot plates baking through and through before the fire, and deep red curtains, ready to be drawn to shut out cold and darkness. *(Stave 3)*

Activity 4

1. With a partner, find examples of Dickens's presentation of each of the following:
   - physical light – either natural or artificial
   - symbolic light – where it signifies something else, such as goodness, happiness, etc.
   - physical darkness
   - symbolic darkness – where it signifies something else, such as evil, ignorance, etc.

2. Make a note of any words or phrases that you find especially effective in the way Dickens describes the light or darkness.

3. Write four paragraphs showing the effects of Dickens's presentation of both light and darkness.

Youth and age

Dickens had strong views about childhood, seeing every day the waste of young lives in mines and factories, and as skivvies and beggars. The children he shows in his story have different experiences and it is clear which the author prefers. He shows the ragged boy who is chased away by Scrooge for singing a carol; the trials of Tiny Tim, crippled by an illness that could be cured if money was available; the feral state of the representatives of Ignorance and Want; and the sad neglect of Scrooge himself as a boy. In contrast to these social victims are the children who are healthy and loved, like those of Belle and her husband in Stave 2 and the other members of the Cratchit family. Childhood should be a time for games and laughter, especially at Christmas; as the narrator says, **'it is good to be children sometimes, and never better than at Christmas, when its mighty Founder was a child himself'** *(Stave 3)*. Dickens never forgot his own dreadful childhood experiences in a debtors' prison and the shoe blacking factory.

When Scrooge is taken back to his past, there is a description of the school, which Dickens no doubt intended as a criticism of many similar establishments where children were sent to be 'educated' and were often forgotten: **'entering the dreary hall, and glancing through the open doors of many rooms, they found them poorly furnished, cold, and vast. There was an earthy savour in the air, a chilly bareness in the place, which associated itself somehow with too much getting up by candle-light, and not too much to eat'** *(Stave 2)*. The standard of schooling was another target of Dickens's reforming instincts and the description here implies some of the miseries suffered by boys like Ebenezer. Here time hangs heavy for the neglected child left in school on his own during the Christmas holidays with only his reading books to keep him company.

Age is represented in the tale mainly by Scrooge and by Marley, dead for seven years. The old grandfather in the mining family, shown by the Ghost of Christmas

Present, is frail but happy in his extended family. He is an opposite of the miser, whose chosen solitude keeps him away from pleasure and from people. When he is given the chance to look back on his childhood, Scrooge begins to feel emotions and when he hears his niece, Fred's wife, play a tune that his sister used to play, **'all the things that Ghost had shown him, came upon his mind; he softened more and more; and thought that if he could have listened to it often, years ago, he might have cultivated the kindnesses of life for his own happiness with his own hands'** *(Stave 3)*. This sorrow at his own lost childhood is the start of his rebirth as a better person.

> **Key quotations**
>
> **Then the shouting and the struggling, and the onslaught that was made on the defenceless porter! The scaling him with chairs for ladders to dive into his pockets, despoil him of brown-paper parcels, hold on tight by his cravat, hug him round his neck, pommel his back, and kick his legs in irrepressible affection! The shouts of wonder and delight with which the development of every package was received!** *(Stave 2)*
>
> **They were a boy and girl. Yellow, meagre, ragged, scowling, wolfish; but prostrate, too, in their humility.** *(Stave 3)*

> **Activity 5**
>
> With a partner, look at Dickens's use of antithesis, or contrast, in the following sections of the novella:
>
> - Stave 1 – the meeting between Scrooge and his nephew (contrast between youth and age)
> - Stave 1 – the meeting between Scrooge and Marley's Ghost (contrast between the physical and the supernatural)
> - Stave 1 – Scrooge's treatment of Bob Cratchit, and Stave 2 – Fezziwig's treatment of Scrooge (contrast between greed and generosity)
> - Stave 1 – Scrooge's apartment, and Stave 3 – his room transformed by the spirit (contrast between light and dark).
>
> Discuss and make notes on how Dickens presents these contrasts and their effects.

Christmas

Dickens himself loved Christmas and saw it as an important time for families to be together. The way it is portrayed in the novella shows it to be a time for coming together for feasting, music, dancing and playing games whatever one's social background or income. In the novella we are shown how the Cratchit family comes together for Christmas and manages to have a dinner of goose and pudding despite a low income. In contrast, Fred is shown at a large family party with a splendid dinner and many guests playing music and party games, but at heart these celebrations are very similar. Both raise a toast to Scrooge, despite his bad behaviour, because forgiveness is seen as part of the festival spirit: **"A Merry Christmas and a Happy New Year to the old man, whatever he is!" said Scrooge's nephew. "He wouldn't take it from me, but may he have it, nevertheless. Uncle Scrooge!"** *(Stave 3).*

The Ghost of Christmas Past shows both the lonely young Ebenezer in his schoolroom at Christmas and his enjoyment of Fezziwig's ball. This contrast pinpoints what Christmas ought to be. Scrooge's former fiancée Belle is shown playing games with her children and we see their joyful rush to discover what presents their father has brought

The Fezziwigs' Christmas ball

home. When Scrooge is taken on his long journey with the Ghost of Christmas Present, Dickens shows Christmas being enjoyed even in the most unlikely places: a lighthouse and a boat out at sea, where **'every man on board, waking or sleeping, good or bad, had had a kinder word for another on that day than on any day in the year; and had shared to some extent in its festivities; and had remembered those he cared for at a distance, and had known that they delighted to remember him'** *(Stave 3).*

Dickens shows the bustle of preparation for the day with the shops glowing with light and festive goods: **'the raisins were so plentiful and rare, the almonds so extremely white, the sticks of cinnamon so long and straight, the other spices so delicious, the candied fruits so caked and spotted with molten sugar'** *(Stave 3).* The listing of the food items and the repetition of the word 'so' highlight the excitement and sense of abundance that characterizes the season.

Dickens also shows Christmas as a time of religious observance as **'the steeples called good people all, to church and chapel, and away they came, flocking through the streets in their best clothes, and with their gayest faces'** *(Stave 3).* Bob Cratchit and Tiny Tim are among their number.

Christmas is presented as a time for sharing and for giving generously to those who were worse off; as Fred says, **"as a good time; a kind, forgiving, charitable, pleasant time; the only time I know of, in the long calendar of the year, when men and women seem by one consent to open their shut-up hearts freely"** (*Stave 1*). He is followed immediately by the two charity collectors seeking donations so that the poorest people can participate in some festive cheer: **"Many thousands are in want of common necessaries; hundreds of thousands are in want of common comforts, sir"** (*Stave 1*).

Scrooge's attitude towards Christmas is Dickens's way of revealing his character. The fact that he refuses to celebrate, or even acknowledge, a season of goodwill and festivity points to someone who is incapable of feeling and cut off from his fellow human beings. He slinks away into the darkness while others are lighting fires and candles to decorate their homes and drawing their curtains **'to shut out cold and darkness'** (*Stave 3*). In a society where most people see Christmas as a special time to remember their common humanity a man like Scrooge stands out.

Dickens uses Christmas Eve to present a parable: a moral story of an evil man who is redeemed by the spirit of Christmas. The feast that Christians remember as the birth of the saviour, who **redeemed** mankind, is seen as an appropriate period to show the redemption of one man.

> **redeem** in Christian terms, to save a person from sin and make them better

Activity 6

How does Dickens present Christmas in each of the following extracts?

a) Stave 2 – Fezziwig's ball
b) Stave 2 – the home of Belle and her children
c) Stave 3 – the Cratchit family's Christmas
d) Stave 3 – Fred's Christmas party

Families

The importance of a loving family is clearly presented by Dickens in *A Christmas Carol*. His own childhood was far from happy, but he was part of a family and close to his sister, Fanny. He shows a clear contrast between Scrooge, who rejects his sister's family in a very ill-natured manner, and his nephew Fred. Fred encourages the family to join him for Christmas dinner, where **'being thoroughly good-natured, and not much caring what they laughed at, so that they laughed at any rate, he encouraged them in their merriment, and passed the bottle joyously'** (*Stave 3*).

In Stave 2, when Scrooge is reminded of his broken engagement, he is shown Belle's family, in particular her eldest daughter, and **'when he thought that such another creature, quite as graceful and as full of promise, might have called him father, and been a spring-time in the haggard winter of his life, his sight grew very dim indeed'**. Thus Dickens shows Scrooge regretting his decision to ignore love in pursuit of money, giving up the chance of a family to follow his own selfish way.

Scrooge treats his clerk Bob Cratchit badly, knowing and caring nothing about his home life, until he is shown by the Ghost of Christmas Present what a close and loving family the Cratchits are. They are happy in spite of their lack of money and their sadness about the illness of Tiny Tim. They make the most of what they have and are thankful to be together for their Christmas feast, although it is a very small goose and a little pudding. They are seen together in Stave 4, after the 'death' of Tiny

Bob Cratchit and Tiny Tim

Tim, being no less close and loving despite their unhappiness. Dickens uses them as an example of moral behaviour, uncomplaining, hard-working and supporting each other in good times and bad: **"But however and whenever we part from one another, I am sure we shall none of us forget poor Tiny Tim – shall we – or this first parting that there was among us?"** *(Stave 4)*.

Dickens shows families such as Fezziwig's, who are well-off but open their doors to everyone in celebrating Christmas. Fezziwig and his family serve as an important model for Scrooge. Fezziwig demonstrates that one does not need to be isolated, selfish or cold-hearted in order to be a successful businessman – something that Scrooge begins to realize over the course of the night.

These families are balanced against those, such as the young Scrooge's, who choose to abandon their children in schools or workhouses, and those children who are left to roam the streets and fall into crime or die of starvation and neglect like those under the Ghost's robe. In a society where there was little provision for the poor and unemployed, or for orphans, good families were a protection, providing nurturing, education and assistance with employment.

Activity 7

Examine the following quotations. How do they contribute to Dickens's presentation of family life in the novella?

- 'Scrooge took his melancholy dinner in his usual melancholy tavern; and having read all the newspapers, and beguiled the rest of the evening with his banker's-book, went home to bed.' *(Stave 1)*

- 'There were more dances, and there were forfeits, and more dances, and there was cake, and there was negus, and there was a great piece of Cold Roast, and there was a great piece of Cold Boiled, and there were mince-pies, and plenty of beer.' *(Stave 2)*

- "One Christmas time, when yonder solitary child was left here all alone, he did come, for the first time, just like that." *(Stave 2)*

- 'Then all the Cratchit family drew round the hearth, in what Bob Cratchit called a circle, meaning half a one; and at Bob Cratchit's elbow stood the family display of glass.' *(Stave 3)*

- 'The ways were foul and narrow; the shops and houses wretched; the people half-naked, drunken, slipshod, ugly.' *(Stave 4)*

- '... they had just had dinner; and, with the dessert upon the table, were clustered round the fire, by lamplight.' *(Stave 3)*

Writing about themes

Upgrade

The way you approach themes in your exam will depend on the question you have been asked. You may be asked to focus on a particular theme, such as Christmas, family life, poverty or the supernatural. In this case, you need to show how Dickens brings out these themes in the novella through different characters, events, the narration and language.

Even if the question does not specifically ask you about themes, you should still show that you have understood them. For example, if you are writing about the character of Bob Cratchit, you could show how Dickens presents themes of Christmas, poverty, the family and childhood through the way he describes Bob and his wife and children.

You should also look at how the themes develop as the novella continues. For example, are we shown more levels of poverty as the story goes on? Is the theme of the family more important at the end of the novella than at the beginning, especially to Scrooge? Do certain events contribute more to the theme of redemption than others?

Exam skills

Understanding the question

Try to approach the question in a methodical way. Start by identifying what the question is actually asking you to do. You could do this by underlining the key words and phrases in the question and writing in what they mean. Exam questions include certain words and phrases that are used quite often. Learn what they mean and that will tell you what you need to write about.

You may be given an extract from the novella in the exam and asked to use it in your answer, as well as referring to the rest of the novella. If this is the case, you will be expected to refer in detail to the extract, quoting where appropriate. You should be selective in how you use the rest of the novella, making sure that your chosen references and quotations are relevant to the question. For example, if you are asked to show how Dickens presents children in the story, then you should make sure that your chosen references are related to children, rather than, say, ghosts.

Explore means look at all the different aspects of something. For example, 'Explore the significance of families...' means you need to look at how families are portrayed in the novella: why families are shown as they are and whether they are important or not; how families are shown and what response is made to them by Scrooge at different places in the story; and how important family, or lack of it, is to the plot, structure and themes of the story.

How does the author... or **show how...** means explain the techniques the author uses to gain their effects. For example, 'How does Dickens make this episode tense?' means you need to look at how he builds up suspense or tension in the way he structures the episode; how he uses language such as verbs and descriptions to make the reader feel the excitement or fear; and how he uses the reactions of the characters in the scene to make the reader see, hear and feel what they see, hear and feel.

Present and **portray** are similar words for looking at a character and prompt you to consider not only what the character is like, but also what devices the author uses to show this. For example, 'How is Scrooge presented / portrayed?' means you need to say how he is described; what Dickens makes him say and do, and why; how Dickens shows other characters reacting to him; and how the writer shows him as important to the story.

In what ways... means look at different sides of something. For example, 'In what ways are the scenes of Scrooge's youth important to the story?' means you should examine how these scenes affect Scrooge himself; the effect on the reader; and whether it gives you a greater sympathy with and understanding of Scrooge or not.

How far... means show the extent of something. For example, in 'How far is child poverty significant in the story?' you would need to demonstrate the different ways in which Dickens reveals his feelings about the lack of education, child labour, illness and other afflictions that affect the children in the novella. You should also write about how he portrays children who do not appear to be poor or ignorant and are not made to work for their living, and what this contrast suggests.

What role... means write not just about the character and how they are shown but also about their function in the novella. For example, 'What role does Tiny Tim have in the novella?' means you need to write about his character and how it is shown, but also why he is in the novella at all. You would need to imagine the novella without him: he is an intelligent and sensitive child who is aware of his disability but manages it as best he can; he is much loved but destined to die because Bob cannot afford medical treatment for him; as well as showing the unfairness of society, he has a profound effect on Scrooge, which you should examine.

Explain or **comment on** are phrases that invite you to give your response to something in as much detail as you can. For example, 'Explain the importance of the ghosts in the novella' means you should write about the way in which Marley's Ghost is a catalyst for change, which is further prompted by the three spirits of Christmas. Without this supernatural intervention, it is very unlikely that Scrooge would have altered his life and instead the future shown by the final spirit would have come to pass.

Examining the question

Look at the question below. The key words and phrases have been highlighted and explained.

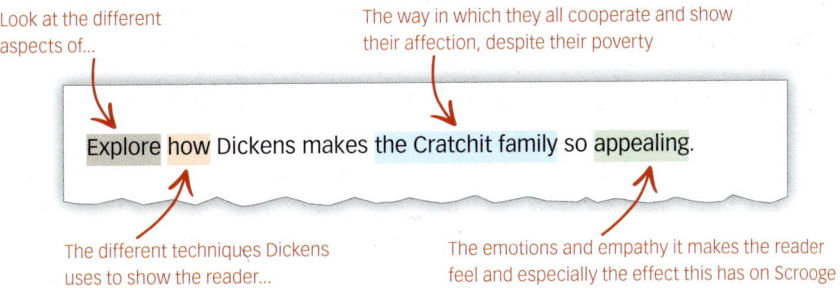

Look at the different aspects of...

The way in which they all cooperate and show their affection, despite their poverty

Explore how Dickens makes the Cratchit family so appealing.

The different techniques Dickens uses to show the reader...

The emotions and empathy it makes the reader feel and especially the effect this has on Scrooge

You can see that you are being asked to do a number of things in this question. What you need to look at is:

- how Dickens brings out the relationship between the Cratchits
- how he shows the reader the family's feelings
- how he shows the complete opposite of Scrooge's wealth and attitudes
- how Dickens makes the reader aware of the way they help to change Scrooge.

Activity 1

1. Write out the following question.

> **Explore the importance of Christmas in the novella as a whole.**

   a) Highlight or underline the key words and phrases. Then describe what you are being asked to do.

   b) Make a list of things you need to do to answer the question.

2. Work with a partner and imagine you are the Chief Examiner. Write two or three questions that you think would test the assessment objectives for this part of the exam. Try to word them as they would be on an actual paper. Check your exam board's website to find example questions and a list of assessment objectives.

3. Swap with another pair and analyse each other's questions as in the example above.

Tips for assessment

To gain the higher grades in the exam, you need to show that you have thought about the novella for yourself and can give your own opinions about what the author is saying and how he is saying it, supporting your ideas with references and quotations.

Planning your answer

It is worth taking five minutes to plan your answer before you start to write. It means you will have the information you need in front of you and you will have some kind of structure. You will be free to concentrate on your writing style and make sure you have used the correct terminology and included evidence to support your points.

Examiners always make the point that candidates who use their own ideas about the text produce fresher and more interesting answers than candidates who have prepared essays in advance. So, the key is to practise planning answers to a variety of questions and, if you want to write practice answers, not to learn them by heart!

The most useful thing about a plan is that you can jot down ideas quickly and then concentrate on writing your answer as well as you can. It is best not to spend more than five minutes doing this.

When planning your response in the exam, you can make a list of points you want to include, perhaps with a brief note of the evidence you will use. Look at the question and bullet point plan on the next page.

> **Explore the importance of Christmas in the extract from Stave 1, from "Don't be cross, uncle!" to 'extinguished the last frail spark for ever', and in the novella as a whole.**

Bullet point plan

1. Scrooge: Christmas an excuse for spending money you don't have
   - people who consider it important are fools
   - he wants to be left alone, without Christmas
2. Fred: Christmas important feast – birth of Christ
   - kind, forgiving time
   - time for thinking of others – the poor
   - emotional and spiritual gain – financial loss OK
3. Two opposite views – until ghosts work their magic
   - Scrooge revisits the past, sees happy families in the present and sees what the future holds – sees Fred is right and Christmas is important
   - He realizes giving to others and close family = joy and satisfaction – not just at Christmas

Spider diagram plan

You could also use a simple spider diagram to plan your points.

You could add more bullet points or boxes in the form of references and quotations as you think of them.

Activity 2

1. Create either a bullet point plan or a spider diagram plan for this question:

   How does Dickens present children and childhood in *A Christmas Carol*?

   Look at the passage at the end of Stave 3 where Scrooge is shown the children under the Ghost's robe. How does Dickens present the effect of poverty on children here and in the rest of the novella?

2. In groups of two or three, compare the plans you have created. Exchange ideas and add to or amend your plan as necessary. Add stars next to what you consider to be the most important points in each plan. Be prepared to discuss your ideas with the class.

Activity 3

Work in a group of four and take one of the following questions each. Use either a spider diagram or a bullet point list to plan an answer to your question.

- In what ways does Dickens show how Scrooge changes throughout the novella?
- Do you think family life is important in the novella? Give reasons for your answer.
- Look at Marley's Ghost and its visitation in Stave 1. How well does this set the scene for everything that happens afterwards?
- How does Dickens present ideas about giving in *A Christmas Carol*?

Share and discuss your plan with the rest of your group.

Tips for assessment

- Plan your time carefully in the exam. Don't spend too long on your plan or you will run out of time to complete your answer.
- Don't cross out your plan because if you do run out of time you may be given credit for it.

Writing your answer

When writing your answer, you should start with a brief introduction, develop your argument point by point, supported by references and quotations, and finish with a conclusion that does not merely repeat the introduction, but takes it further.

For example, in the question about the importance of Christmas on page 77:

- your introduction might show the disagreement between Scrooge and his nephew, and say why and how Dickens presents it
- your development would show how the author portrays the differing effects on Scrooge of each of the ghostly visits

- in the conclusion, you might say that Scrooge has now come to see Fred's viewpoint but also that he now practises the 'Christmas' virtues all the time.

You also need to pay close attention to the quality of your writing, including your spelling, grammar and punctuation. Your answer should show your knowledge and understanding of:

- what the author is saying
- how the author is saying it
- briefly, how the setting and the context influence the writer and reader (if context is assessed as part of your exam).

Using Point, Evidence, Explanation (PEE)

Examiners want to see that you are able to support your ideas in a thoughtful way and that you have based them on what the writer says and means. For example, you might make the point:

> The clinching argument for Scrooge to change his ways at once is the sight of his gravestone.

Your evidence for this might be:

> "I will honour Christmas in my heart, and try to keep it all the year. I will live in the Past, the Present, and the Future. The Spirits of all Three shall strive within me. I will not shut out the lessons that they teach. Oh, tell me I may sponge away the writing on this stone!" (Stave 4)

Your explanation might be:

> This shows clearly that Scrooge has taken the night's lessons to heart and the softening that began when he remembered his childhood is finally complete when he fears it may be too late. His mental and emotional agony at this point is not in doubt and his anxiety that he may not have time to make amends is an assurance of his reform.

Tips for assessment

While it is helpful to use PEE as a guide, do not follow it for every single point you make, only for the important ones, otherwise you may get bogged down rather than keeping your answer flowing.

Using quotations

This is an important part of using evidence in your answer. The examiner will want to see that you are able to select appropriate quotations that back up the point you are making. When you make a point ask yourself, 'How do I know this?' Usually it will be because of something the author has written: this is the quotation you need.

For example, you might make the point

> The Cratchits are a kind and loving family.

How do you know this? Well there might be a number of quotations you could choose, but here is one:

> 'Martha didn't like to see him disappointed, if it were only in joke; so she came out prematurely from behind the closet door, and ran into his arms' (Stave 3)

By choosing this quotation, you will show several things:

- that you can select a relevant quotation to support your answer
- that you have understood how the family all help each other
- that you have understood that this relates to an important aspect of family life.

Examiners will reward you for using well-chosen quotations in your answer, but if you want to show higher level skills you need to try to use 'embedded quotations'. These are quotations that are used as part of the main text, marked out only by speech marks.

You can use this technique for short quotations. For example:

> Without Marley's Ghost it is doubtful that Scrooge would have changed, because the spectre tells him that he has come "to warn you, that you have yet a chance and hope of escaping my fate" (Stave 1). This is Marley's one decent legacy to his old partner and friend.

You will not be expected to remember long quotations or a large number of them in a closed book exam, but you should try to learn a few shorter quotations that you could use in different contexts.

You should make use of the printed extract on the paper for suitable quotations wherever possible.

There are some famous quotations, such as "Bah! Humbug!" (Stave 1) as Scrooge's response to Christmas, or "God bless us every one!" (Stave 3) from Tiny Tim, that you should know.

What not to do in an exam answer

✗ Do not begin with introductions such as 'In this answer I am going to show...'. Just start your answer and do the showing as you go. Make sure your introduction addresses the question and go back to the question in your conclusion.

✗ Do not write lengthy paragraphs about the background to the novella. You may think that Victorian attitudes to poverty are important in understanding the novella, but you should show this while you are answering the question itself.

✗ Do not focus on some parts of the set extract and ignore others. You should always answer on the extract as a whole.

✗ Do not write a long introduction showing what you know about the author. This should be a brief reference, and only used if it is relevant to a point you are making. For example, you may think Dickens's experiences in the shoe blacking factory had a profound effect on the way he shows the poor throughout the novella, but mention this as briefly as possible.

✗ Do not go into the exam with a prepared list of points, which may not be relevant to the question, and then write about them regardless of the focus of the question!

✗ Do not 'feature spot' in the set extract. There is little merit in saying that Dickens uses symbolism without showing how he does this and what effect it creates.

✗ Do not run out of time to finish your answer – a plan will help you to avoid this.

✗ It is better to focus on a detailed answer on a small part of the text than to try and make lots of different points.

✗ Do not try to write everything you know about the text. Make sure you choose things that are relevant to the question.

Achieving the best marks

Upgrade

If you have read the tips for assessment so far, you will have some idea of the standard you need to reach to achieve good marks in the exam. To reach the highest grades, you will need to:

- show an assured or perceptive understanding of themes, characters, setting and literary techniques
- show a suitable or convincing response to the text, including appropriate use of subject terminology
- make sure your selection of evidence is relevant, detailed and consistent, as well as integrated
- if required, include references to context that are appropriate, convincing and supported by relevant textual reference
- write sentences that are sophisticated and varied; show good control of expression and meaning; use a full range of punctuation and accurate spelling.

You need to show that you have understood the novella on more than one level. On the surface, it is a story about how a mean old miser is reformed by some ghosts and becomes a new man. On an underlying level, it is a criticism of society and the way in which it fails to promote equality and freedom for all and, in particular, it is a criticism of the treatment of the poorest and most vulnerable people. On a still deeper level, it is a novella about the human condition, the way in which evil is associated with greed and isolation from human warmth, while good comes from caring and forgiveness.

You need to show that you understand the way in which the narrative works and why Dickens chooses to use a narrator's viewpoint, although it follows Scrooge so closely. You will also need to show, not just that you have understood the symbolism that Dickens uses, but how, in your view, he applies it and why he uses it.

In addition, you will need to use the correct literary terminology to make your answers more precise and show that you have a sophisticated writing style.

Sample questions

1

Read the extract from Stave 3 beginning "And how did little Tim behave?" to 'and feebly cried Hurrah!'

In this extract, Scrooge is taken by the Ghost of Christmas Present to visit the Cratchit family. Starting with this extract, how does Dickens present Cratchit family life? Write about:

- how Dickens presents the Cratchit family and their relationships in this extract
- how Dickens presents the Cratchit family and their relationships in the novella as a whole.

2

Read the extract from Stave 1 beginning 'The apparition walked backward from him' to 'fell asleep upon the instant'. You should use the extract and your knowledge of the whole novella to answer this question.

Explore how Dickens uses ghosts to bring about the change in Scrooge. In your response you should:

- refer to the extract and the novella as a whole
- show your understanding of characters and events in the novella
- refer to the contexts of the novella.

3

Read the extract from Stave 3 beginning 'The Grocers'! oh the Grocers'!' to "Because it needs it most".

a) Explore how Dickens portrays attitudes towards Christmas in this extract and elsewhere in the novella.
Give examples from the novella to support your ideas.

b) Explore how Dickens presents attitudes towards Christmas elsewhere in the novella.

In your answer you must consider:
- the different celebrations that are shown
- how Christmas affects those involved.

4

Read the extract from Stave 3 beginning 'The chimes were ringing the three quarters past eleven at that moment' to 'The bell struck twelve'. Then answer the question that follows.

How does Dickens present poverty and neglect in the novella?
Write about:
- how Dickens presents poverty and neglect in this extract
- how Dickens presents poverty and neglect in the novella as a whole.

5

Read the extract from Stave 1 beginning 'Oh! But he was a tight-fisted hand at the grindstone, Scrooge!' to 'They often 'came down' handsomely, and Scrooge never did'. You should use the extract and your knowledge of the whole novella to answer this question.

Write about how Dickens presents Scrooge and the change to his character throughout the novella.

In your response you should:
- refer to the extract and the novella as a whole
- show your understanding of characters and events in the novella
- refer to the contexts of the novella.

6

Read the extract from Stave 2 beginning 'The Spirit touched him on the arm' to "I should like to have given him something: that's all".

a) Explore how Dickens presents childhood and education in this extract. Give examples from the extract to support your ideas.

b) In this extract, childhood is shown. Explain how Dickens portrays childhood elsewhere in the novella.

In your answer you must consider:
- the childhood experiences that are shown
- how their childhood experiences affect those involved.

Activity 4

Choose one of the sample questions. Make a plan for your answer, using one of the methods shown in the planning section on pages 76–77.

Find another student who has chosen the same question and exchange notes and ideas.

Activity 5

Work with a partner, using the plan you made for your chosen sample question. Choose one of the points you identified in your plan and write down how you would use PEE in your answer to show skills in selecting and evaluating evidence.

Compare your use of PEE with others in the class and decide if you would change or modify your own response.

Sample answers

Sample answer 1

Below is an extract from a sample answer by a student, together with examiner comments, to the following question on the novella.

> Read the extract from Stave 1 beginning 'After several turns, he sat down again' to 'could see the two buttons on his coat behind'.
>
> How does Dickens use suspense to introduce the ghosts
> - in the printed extract?
> - in the novella as a whole?

In the extract it is the ghost of Scrooge's old partner, Marley, who appears. We are told he is 'as dead as a door-nail' at the beginning of Stave 1, which shows his passing in rather facetious terms. Dickens writes at length about his death, so that when Scrooge sees his face suddenly in the door knocker it is unexpected, but also prepares the reader for further strange events. After this sight, and that of a mysterious hearse preceding Scrooge up the stairs, Dickens then uses the sense of hearing to increase suspense as Scrooge sits in his room. He is unsettled at the start of the extract for we are told that 'after several turns he sat down again' and Dickens builds on this unease when he describes the disused bell starting to ring, increasing in volume and being joined by all the other bells in the house. This fills Scrooge with 'a strange, inexplicable dread', which is also felt by the reader. The next increase in tension comes as the bells stop ringing, but are succeeded by 'a clanking noise' in the cellar. The writer then tells of the chains being dragged up the stairs towards Scrooge's room. His attempt to bolster his courage by saying it is 'humbug' merely adds to the scariness and by the time the Ghost walks through the locked door we wonder what we will see.

Dickens has tightened the tension like a screw up to this point, but then he uses bathos for his description of the Ghost, who looks 'the very same' as in life except that he is transparent and there is a slightly comic touch about the fact that Scrooge can see the two buttons on the back of his coat. The scene continues with the author alternating between horror, such as when the Ghost removes its bandage and its jaw falls, and humour, especially from Scrooge who makes facetious comments such as 'You're particular, for a shade' and tells it he thinks it is a product of indigestion. It is made clear to the reader, however, that Scrooge is using humour as a way of 'keeping down his terror'. However, by the time the Ghost leaves, Scrooge

Marginal examiner comments:

Shows awareness of humour as well as tension in the Ghost's appearance.

Perceptive comments on use of the senses to create suspense.

Well-integrated quotation that is also relevant.

Makes a connection between Scrooge's viewpoint and the reader's reactions.

A succinct and well-written summary of Dickens's increase of tension

Well-observed use of bathos as a comic technique.

Evaluation of Dickens's use of humour and horror.

realizes he will be in the same position very soon unless he allows the three spirits foretold by Marley to help him. The turning point in the encounter is when the Ghost, in response to Scrooge's compliment about being a good 'man of business' cries out in anguish, 'Mankind was my business', and Dickens shows the torment of those who realize, too late, what they should have done during their time on Earth. The final part is rather touching with the unfortunate wandering spirits unable to help a poor woman with a baby.

Intelligent awareness of the purpose of the Ghost and Dickens's use of sentiment.

The three spirits who visit Scrooge over the course of the night are all different. The first represents Memory, as the Ghost of Christmas Past. He is preceded by bells as well, this time the clocks, which Dickens shows chiming very odd hours up to midnight. Again he breaks the tension with bathos by having Scrooge in a fever of expectation waiting for his visitor, only to remember that it was supposed to arrive at one o'clock. He lies awake and is ready to believe it is not coming, when it suddenly draws back his bed curtain, making him start. Dickens describes the Ghost's appearance in some detail, as it has elements of youth and age, winter and summer, light and dark and seems at one moment 'dissolving parts, no outline... visible in the dense gloom' and the next moment clearly visible. This is how memory works but the author makes it very disconcerting both for Scrooge and for the reader.

Good point about the past being representative of memory.

Shows understanding of Dickens's techniques and their similarity to the previous spirit.

Evaluative comments on how the Ghost reflects the nature of memory.

Dickens uses tension in a different way for the appearance of the second spirit, as Scrooge, woken by the clock, puts back the bed curtains himself, so as not to be surprised. However, when nothing happens, he is taken by surprise and starts to tremble. This time he is forced to go in search of the Ghost, whose presence is announced by a flood of light around his room. This is a different kind of light from that of memory, as it permeates the area. When he is drawn to its source, it is his own room transformed into a place of warmth and sparkle. The Ghost is dressed in a loose robe and seated on a mountain of food, while a huge fire flames in the grate. Everything suggests openness and generosity of spirit as well as material goods. The room is the opposite of the one Scrooge has left, with its tiny fire and bowl of gruel, and pinched and miserable occupant. The Ghost himself as described as a 'jolly giant' who holds up the horn of plenty and calls out to Scrooge to join him. The suspense here lies in seeing Scrooge's reaction to such excess and in wondering what kind of a journey he will undergo this time.

Clear understanding of different kinds of tension and how they work.

Good awareness of the Ghost and Scrooge as opposites.

Perceives differing uses of suspense, not just fear.

The student shows a perceptive and thoughtful awareness of how Dickens uses suspense in different ways to present each of the ghosts. There is clear analysis and some attempt at evaluation of techniques, and correct use of literary terminology. Quotations are well chosen and integrated, and the answer is well written.

Sample answer 2

Below is an extract from a sample answer by a student, together with examiner comments, to the following question on the novella.

> Read the extract from Stave 2 beginning 'They were in another scene and place' to "remove me from this place".
>
> How does Dickens present ideas about childhood in *A Christmas Carol*? You should use the extract and your knowledge of the whole novella to answer this question.

The candidate shows understanding of context and the reason for the scene.

This extract shows the life Scrooge might have had with his girlfriend Belle if he had not loved money more than her. When he sees her happy life with her husband and children he cannot bear it and tells the Ghost to take him away. The children are very noisy and excited because of Christmas but their father comes home with lots of presents for them and they climb all over him and are generally a bit wild until they finally go to bed.

Awareness of this aspect of childhood as the fortunate one.

These children are the lucky ones who have money and toys and parents who love them.

Well-chosen and integrated quotation although it could have been evaluated.

I know this because it says that nobody minds them being so loud and rough but 'the mother and daughter laughed heartily, and enjoyed it very much'.

Shows the candidate understands Dickens's purpose, although more analysis required.

I think Dickens puts them in the story to show how some children had better lives and how Scrooge might have been a father if he had not been so fixated on making money.

Clear reason for choosing the Cratchits but rather superficial comments.

A different family Dickens shows in the novella is the Cratchit family. Bob Cratchit is Scrooge's clerk and he treats him badly, not letting him have a fire when it is freezing and paying him small wages.

Some grasp of the Cratchit situation but little analysis of Dickens's technique or purpose.

But even without a lot of money the Cratchit family have a good time at Christmas, although with a small goose and a tiny Christmas pudding and no proper presents.

Good observations of children working but little attempt to analyse Dickens's view.

The children here have to work, all except Tiny Tim, who is too little and who is crippled. The oldest girl Martha is an apprentice to a milliner and is making hats all day every day, except for Christmas when she comes home. Her parents are very happy to see her and so are her brothers and sisters. Peter is the oldest boy and is looking for a job, but all the children help with getting the dinner ready.

Aware that it affects Scrooge, but little evaluation of Dickens's purpose.

They have a happy time together in spite of having no money. This makes it sad that the Ghost tells Scrooge that Tiny Tim will die because they cannot afford medical treatment for his condition. He says he sees an empty seat 'and a crutch without an owner', and this makes Scrooge think.

Not all the children in the story are happy because the Ghost shows Scrooge two scraggy children who are Want and Ignorance, which is a personification of the kind of problems many children had in Dickens's time. Lots of children had to work long days in mines or factories and were often injured or beaten. Lots of children never went to school so they could not improve themselves or their lives. The Ghost says society should beware of these children for they will destroy it. When Scrooge asks if there is nowhere they can go, the Ghost reminds him what he said about workhouses and prisons. He is giving Scrooge a guilt trip here.

Dickens also shows Scrooge's own childhood when the Ghost of Christmas Past takes him back to the school where he was left all on his own in the Christmas holidays, when the others were out playing and enjoying themselves. This must have been very hard for him and maybe explains a bit why he says 'Bah, humbug' about Christmas. He only has books to keep him company and misses out on all the fun.

Use of literary term and attempt to show Dickens's purpose.

Grasp of context but needed to relate it to story.

Useful comment about Dickens's social views and purpose in story.

Thoughtful use of Scrooge's past, related to the question.

Fair attempt to explain the possible reason for Scrooge's attitude, which could have been pursued.

This candidate has engaged with the story and shows a fair understanding of some of Dickens's reasons for including different experiences of childhood. There is also some perception of the effect on Scrooge of these scenes. There is some attempt at analysis and evaluation, but this is not consistent or sustained.

Sample answer 3

Below is an extract from a sample answer by a student, together with examiner comments, to the following question on the novella.

> Read the extract from Stave 5 beginning 'But he was early at the office next morning' to 'God bless Us, Every One!' and then answer the following question.
>
> How does Dickens show Scrooge's character changing? Refer to the extract and to the novella as a whole in your answer.

Sets the extract in the context of the story.

This extract is from the end of the novella, when Scrooge has been redeemed and become someone who is aware of the joys of giving. It begins with him wanting to be in the office before Bob Cratchit, so he can surprise him with his new generous self. He pretends to be the old Scrooge first, to play a trick on Bob before saying, "I am about to raise your salary!" Dickens shows how Bob cannot believe it because he gets closer to the ruler, thinking he can knock Scrooge down and call for help.

Evaluation of language, historical context and purpose supported by integrated quotation.

We know he thinks Scrooge is mad because the narrator refers to a 'strait-waistcoat' (straitjacket), which is used for violently insane people. However, Dickens then shows Scrooge telling him to heap up his fire and inviting him to share a drink while he discusses how 'to assist your struggling family'.

Analysis of language and technique of repetition.

We are shown how Scrooge has reformed forever, because Dickens uses repetition to tell us, writing the word 'good' six times in a sentence so we are in no doubt.

Perceptive contrast with Scrooge as shown at the start of the story.

This new Scrooge has come about over a single night of Christmas. At the start of the novella Scrooge is described as grasping and cold, 'hard as flint' and one who 'carried his own low temperature always about with him'. His attitude towards Christmas is "Bah! Humbug!" and he is rude to his nephew Fred when he invites Scrooge to Christmas dinner.

Succinct and accurate summary of Scrooge's attitude before his change.

He turns away people collecting money for the poor, saying he has to support the workhouses and prisons so they can go there. The collectors protest that people would rather die than go to such dreadful places, but his only response is 'they had better do it, and decrease the surplus population.'

Neat use of rhetorical question to move the answer forward.

So what happens to turn this mean and pinched old miser into the man Dickens shows in the extract?

Thoughtful analysis of the meaning of Marley's Ghost and its description.

The start of his reformation is a visit from the ghost of his former partner Jacob Marley, who is condemned to travel the Earth, in 'an infernal atmosphere' (suggestive of hell), weighed down by chains and unable to do the good deeds he failed to do in his life. Dickens shows him as tormented by this and he tells Scrooge 'I wear the chain I forged in life'. His one good action has been to try and prevent his friend from ending up in the same situation, and therefore he tells Scrooge he will be visited by three spirits, thus creating expectations in the reader. As he floats away, Scrooge sees the air is filled with tormented ghosts seeking to right the wrongs they did in life. Dickens is reminding the reader what Scrooge (or perhaps anyone like him) can expect if he pays no heed to this warning, and also that he has been given an opportunity.

Well-placed comment on Dickens's use of suspense.

Sound evaluation of Dickens's moral and literary purpose.

The Ghost of Christmas Past is Memory, shown by Dickens to be shape-shifting and lit either brightly or dimly at different moments, as is the nature of memories. This Ghost takes Scrooge on a journey back to his own past, which begins the process of reform. It is an emotional journey for Scrooge who shows his first sign of softening when he sheds a tear for his previous, neglected and lonely self. While this has an element of self-pity about it, it is a way for Dickens to reveal the possible origins of Scrooge's attitude towards humanity and Christmas in particular. The author also shows us a child saved from despair by reading and imagination, and gives hope that this child is still somewhere inside Scrooge. The sight of his little sister, whose intervention brought him back to the family home makes Scrooge think of his nephew and perhaps how Fred also wants to include him. A similar recollection about Bob Cratchit is brought home to him as he watches the jolly scene at Fezziwig's. Scrooge finds himself arguing with the Ghost that the importance of Fezziwig was his kindness and thought for his employees and others, rather than any money he spent. He is then struck by the contrast in the way he treats Bob and wishes he could talk to him.

Perceptive on Dickens's technique when describing first spirit.

Analysis of the beginnings of change through the memory of childhood.

Some thoughtful evaluation of Dickens's view of childhood through Scrooge.

Good connection made between 'little Fan' and Fred.

A second connection made between Fezziwig, and Scrooge and Bob.

Scrooge's past life also brings the memory of the break-up between himself and Belle, his fiancée because of his growing worship of money. Dickens shows the pain of this memory as Scrooge begs "No more. I don't wish to see it. Show me no more!" The Ghost, however, presses home the lesson by showing the happy home full of children that Belle now enjoys, while Dickens's narrator tells us that Scrooge's reflection that he could have had a daughter like Belle's makes his sight 'very dim indeed'.

An understanding shown about the role of the Ghost here.

These memories are a way of making Scrooge reflect on how his life might have been if he had made different choices and his reactions show they bring both pain and regret, which are the first steps towards changing.

A brief evaluation of the role of memory in the making of life choices.

Overall, the student has used evaluation and analysis to show the roles of different characters and the author's techniques and purpose in using the ghosts to bring about the changes in Scrooge. There is perceptive understanding of Dickens's moral purpose and of his use of conscience, the past, imagination and memory.

Sample answer 4

Below is an extract from a sample answer by a student, together with examiner comments, to the following question on the novella.

> Read the extract from Stave 2 beginning 'But if they had been twice as many' to "I should like to be able to say a word or two to my clerk just now. That's all".
>
> How does Dickens show the importance of giving in *A Christmas Carol*? You should refer to the printed extract and to the novella as a whole in your answer.

The candidate shows understanding of Dickens's views, although with little attempt at analysis.

There is an implied connection between Dickens's view of giving and Fezziwig.

Accurate understanding of the quotation but it is not integrated or linked to the question.

A sound interpretation of the meaning and an attempt at analysis.

A fair attempt to analyse Scrooge's feelings.

Good contrast with the extract to show Scrooge not giving.

Good understanding of ways in which Scrooge refuses to give, but without much analysis.

Comment shows awareness of purpose and audience.

Charles Dickens thinks Christmas is a time for giving things like presents, and food and money to the poor. In the extract Scrooge is shown when he was an apprentice to a man called Fezziwig who is very jolly and tells the apprentices to shut up early on Christmas Eve so he can give a big dinner and dance for everyone. Fezziwig and his wife are a good pair and they love to dance. I know this because it says 'A positive light appeared to issue from Fezziwig's calves. They shone in every part of the dance like moons.' This means his legs move so fast they twinkle. When the evening is over they make sure to wish everyone a Merry Christmas. Scrooge gets very excited as he watches this scene and remembers how he felt at the time. The Ghost says it is nothing to get excited about as Fezziwig only spent a few pounds on the party, but Scrooge says it is because he could make their lives good or miserable and he chose good. This makes him think about his clerk, Bob Cratchit, and he wishes he could say something to him. Maybe he is feeling a bit guilty because he is so mean to Bob.

At the start of the story Dickens writes about how mean and cold Scrooge is and he won't give anything to anyone – not even a Merry Christmas. He makes his clerk work without a fire in the freezing cold and pays him a low wage. When his nephew invites him for Christmas dinner he says no and tells him to go away. Then he says the same to the charity collectors and won't give them any money to help the poor and needy have a decent Christmas. He also chases away a poor little boy who tries to sing a Christmas carol for him. I think Charles Dickens makes him like this to show people how wrong it is not to be kind and giving, especially at Christmas.

When he is visited by Marley's Ghost, it tells him this behaviour is wrong because he was the same and he has to suffer now he is dead. He shows Scrooge his chain, which is made of all the things to do with money and says Scrooge's will be even longer. He has to wear it and wander about the Earth because he didn't help people when he was alive. He says Scrooge will have visits from three spirits and then he floats out of the window.

Brief account of Marley's Ghost shows relevance to giving and penalties for not giving.

After the spirits have visited and shown Scrooge things like how his old master Fezziwig was kind and giving to him when he was a clerk and how the Cratchits are a family who love and help each other, especially Tiny Tim, Scrooge starts to feel bad about the way he treats Bob. He has a surprise when he enjoys Christmas at Fred's house and wants to stay there but the Ghost won't let him.

Selection of relevant episodes but little comment on the author.

Some reference to Scrooge's feelings but little profound comment.

The candidate shows engagement with the story and Scrooge's feelings. There are some sound comments about the nature of giving and about conscience, but there are few quotations and little attempt at analysis or evaluation. There needed to be more on the way that Dickens presents these things and ideally some knowledge of literary terminology.

Glossary

accumulation of clauses a building up of clauses, one after another; a clause is a part of a sentence that includes a subject and verb and could stand on its own

allegory a story with a second meaning behind the obvious one, using abstract ideas as personified characters

antithesis contrast or opposite

aristocracy those with titles and wealth who owned large estates and stately homes, including members of the royal family

baby farm infants born to single mothers or those unable to care for them were 'fostered' by people (usually women) for a sum of money. The money was not enough to cover the expenses for long and many infants died from neglect

bathos an abrupt change from extraordinary to everyday, giving a comic effect

charwoman a cleaner

cornucopia the horn of plenty, full of a surplus of good things

counting house an accountant's office

debtor a person who owes money

digress to leave the main story in order to make a comment or observation related to something in it, which may be a direct address to the reader

dramatic irony when an audience or reader knows something the characters do not, e.g. when the audience in *Romeo and Juliet* knows that Juliet isn't really dead, but Romeo does not

elevated diction 'high' or complex forms of speech, using precise words and a formal style

empathy the ability to understand someone else's feelings

evangelical revival the reforming of the Church by people who thought it was important to read the Bible and practise good works

Factory Acts a series of Acts of Parliament that set out the working conditions of children and adults in factories

figurative language language that uses 'figures of speech' such as metaphors, similes, personification, repetition, hyperbole, bathos, etc.

first person from the perspective of the main character in the tale, using the pronoun 'I'

foreshadowing a literary technique where the author includes clues for the reader about what will happen later on

gentry the social level just below the aristocracy, whose members owned local manor houses and smaller estates, and sometimes mixed with the aristocracy

gothic a term used to describe stories or poems with a horror or supernatural theme

humanitarianism a viewpoint or philosophy that extends compassion and the relief of suffering to all people regardless of nationality, age, gender or religion

hyperbole exaggeration for the purpose of emphasis

idiolect an individual's unique speech pattern

Industrial Revolution the period from the 18th to the 19th century when goods changed from being made by hand to being made by machines in factories

laundress a woman who washes clothes

Malthus a respected academic and economist who argued that the growth of the world's population would outstrip its ability to provide food for everyone, leading to enforced population control through starvation and disease

metamorphosis one thing changing into another; a transformation

metaphor comparison of one thing to another for effect; a metaphor states that one thing is the other, e.g. 'the cold within him froze his old features'

morality a set of principles and values, concerning what is right and wrong

novella a prose text that is longer than a short story but shorter than a standard novel

oakum tar-covered rope used in shipping; it was picked apart by hand to create fibres

omniscient narrator a storyteller who knows what all the characters are doing, saying and thinking

parable a story related to people's own experiences that illustrates a moral lesson, often through personification and/or metaphor

pathetic fallacy the idea that nature reflects human feelings

personify to give human characteristics to inanimate or abstract ideas or things, e.g. 'Nature lived hard by, and was brewing on a large scale'

phrase a group of words in a sentence that could not form a sentence on their own

Plenty's horn also known as 'Cornucopia', this is a mythical horn filled with everlasting produce

Poor Law a law in England and Wales, amended in 1834, which meant that the rich no longer had to pay taxes in order to help the poor and those affected by poverty had to go into workhouses, which were little better than prisons

protagonist the main character in a work of fiction

qualifiers describing words such as adjectives (which describe nouns) and adverbs (which describe verbs)

Ragged School a school for poor children in cities, offering free education and sometimes clothing and food. This was, for many children, the only education they received. The schools offered reading, writing, arithmetic and Bible studies

redeem in Christian terms, to save a person from sin and make them better

rime deposit of frost

salutary beneficial

satire exposing the failings of people or societies by making fun of them

simile a comparison that shows it is comparing by using 'like' or 'as', e.g. 'solitary as an oyster'

situational irony when the outcome of a situation is the reverse of that intended, e.g. someone being caught in a trap they laid for another person

spiritualism a belief that the spirits of the dead continue to evolve and that it is possible to communicate with them through gifted 'mediums'

stave the set of five lines on which musical notation is written

symbol an object used to represent an idea, e.g. a flag has a symbolic meaning as the representation of a country

third person from the perspective of a character or voice outside the story, using the pronouns 'he' or 'she'

verbal irony words that say the opposite of what someone actually means, e.g. 'What a lovely day!' when it is raining

want a lack of the most basic essentials of life, such as food, shelter and education

workhouse originally set up as a place for the able-bodied unemployed, workhouses provided food and shelter in return for hard labour

OXFORD
UNIVERSITY PRESS

Great Clarendon Street, Oxford, OX2 6DP, United Kingdom

Oxford University Press is a department of the University of Oxford. It furthers the University's objective of excellence in research, scholarship, and education by publishing worldwide. Oxford is a registered trade mark of Oxford University Press in the UK and in certain other countries

© Carmel Waldron 2015

The moral rights of the author have been asserted

First published in 2015

British Library Cataloguing in Publication Data

Data available

ISBN 978-019-835531-1
Kindle edition 978-019-836888-5

10 9 8 7 6 5 4 3

Printed in China by Golden Cup Printing Co Ltd.

Acknowledgements

Cover: © Pabkov/Shutterstock; **p1:** © Pabkov/Shutterstock; **p6:** © The Print Collector/Alamy; **p8:** Copyright Supplied by Capital Pictures; **p10:** © AF archive/Alamy; **p13:** © ClassicStock/Alamy; **p15:** © AF archive/Alamy; **p20:** © Steve Vidler/Alamy; **p23:** Ann Ronan Pictures/Print Collector/Getty Images; **p26:** The Cartoon Collector/Print Collector/Getty Images; **p28:** Col. print aft. painting, 1909, by Franz Bohumil Doubek (born 1865)/akg-images; **p30:** © Moviestore collection Ltd/Alamy; **p34:** Copyright Supplied by Capital Pictures; **p38:** © Steve Ross/Capital Pictures; **p40:** © AF archive/Alamy; **p41:** © Martin Harris/Capital Pictures; **p43:** REX/British Library/Robana; **p47:** Culture Club/Getty Images; **p50:** © Classic Image/Alamy; **p52:** Ann Ronan Pictures/Print Collector/Getty Images; **p55:** © AF archive/Alamy; **p57:** © Steve Ross/Capital Pictures; **p61:** Copyright Supplied by Capital Pictures; **p64:** Culture Club/Getty Images; **p69:** Ann Ronan Pictures/Print Collector/Getty Images; **p71:** © GraphicaArtis/Corbis

Extracts are taken from Charles Dickens: *A Christmas Carol and Other Christmas Books* edited by Robert Douglas-Fairhurst (Oxford World Classics, 2008).